LEARNING DISABILITIES AND THE CHURCH

Including All God's Kids in Your Education and Worship

Cynthia Holder Rich
Martha Ross-Mockaitis

Foreword by Barbara J. Newman

FAITH ALIVE®
Christian Resources

Grand Rapids, Michigan

Learning Disabilities and the Church: Including All God's Kids in Your Education and Worship. © 2006 Faith Alive Christian Resources, 2850 Kalamazoo Ave. SE, Grand Rapids, MI 49560. All rights reserved. Printed in the United States on recycled paper.

We welcome your comments. Call us at 1-800-333-8300 or e-mail us at editors@faithaliveresources.org.

Library of Congress Cataloging-in-Publication Data

Rich, Cynthia Holder.
  Learning disabilities and the church : including all God's kids in your education and worship / Cynthia Holder Rich, Martha Ross-Mockaitis.
     p. cm.
  ISBN 1-59-255-262-5 (alk. paper)
  1. Church work with learning disabled children. 2. Church work with learning disabled youth. I. Ross-Mockaitis, Martha. II. Title.
  BV4461.R53 2006
  259'.4--dc22

                                        2006011696

10 9 8 7 6 5 4 3 2 1

CONTENTS

ABBREVIATIONS

Here is a list of common abbreviations for terms you might hear or read about in the area of Learning Disabilities and Attention-Deficit/Hyperactivity Disorder:

ADA   Americans with Disabilities Act of 1990 (U.S.)

ADD   Attention Deficit Disorder(s). This term was used to distinguish an individual with the inattentive type of Attention-Deficit/Hyperactivity Disorder. You may still hear people use this term, but it is no longer used in the fields of education or psychology.

AD/HD   Attention-Deficit/Hyperactivity Disorder. Includes three different types: AD/HD—Predominantly Inattentive Type; AD/HD—Predominantly Hyperactive-Impulsive Type; or AD/HD—Combined Type.

IDEA   Individuals with Disability Education Act of 2004 (U.S.)

IEP   Individualized Education Program (U.S.)

LD   Learning Disabilities

NCLB   No Child Left Behind Act of 2002 (U.S.)

NIMH   National Institutes of Mental Health (U.S.)

FOREWORD

How do you learn best? If, for example, your spouse asks you to bring home six items from the grocery store, how do you remember that list? Do you grab a piece of paper? Rehearse the list several times in your head? Come up with a quick song or rhyme to help you remember which items your spouse needs to create dinner? Try to picture the finished meal in your head and link that picture with the items needed? What's your learning style?

Perhaps you've never thought about your learning style. I can assure you, however, that you have built your life around it. You simply processed that list of six items without giving much thought to the method you used. You have created successful ways of categorizing, memorizing, learning, retrieving, attending, and speaking—at school, at work, at home. You have surrounded yourself with the tools and methods you need to be successful. Most of us use these strategies effortlessly each day—that is, until we hit a snag.

Now imagine that you've been given a list of six items to purchase—but you find yourself without paper and pencil. Suddenly you need to find an alternate method for remembering the list. So you try to visualize the needed items—only to discover that you are in such a noisy environment that you can't focus. Or imagine that you need to schedule an appointment but your planner's in the car. Or your computer is down and you can't access your schedule. It's time to come up with Plan B. This is something of a chore. You actually need to think about how you will remember or execute something.

Frustrating as they are, those are the times you can best relate to individuals who struggle with memory and recall. Those are the moments that remind you that some things you normally do effortlessly may be more difficult for others.

Although this book is about children who have been labeled "learning disabled," it's important to place that term in context. It's important to explore your own unique learning package as well as to examine how other image-bearers of God learn. It's important to shift gears into that place we sometimes call Plan B.

Most schools and churches are set up for a "one size fits all" approach. I have the distinct advantage of being packaged in a body that learns by ear and can process language well through speaking and writing. Most schools and churches are set up for people who are wired like me. We listen to sermons or lectures. We respond by discussing in small groups or by completing written assignments. But what about the person who is wired to learn best through visual examples? What about the person who can think in pictures and draw an in-depth portrait of the message or lesson? Although I was typically rewarded in school with "A"s, my friend who excelled in visual images was not. Does that make my friend disabled?

Let's turn the tables for a moment. Let's imagine that sermons are a series of visual images not connected with words. Let's imagine that every assignment requires you to create a well-thought-out painting conveying the main idea and content of the lesson. Who would be the "disabled" one now? Let's face it: we have set up our learning environments for the success of those who flourish in the most typical presentation and response modes. The others are generally out of luck.

We live in a time when differences are quickly labeled. People with unique medical conditions and learning differences often have initials or categories attached to their names. A child may have AD/HD. An adult may have Cerebral Palsy (CP). In a way, these designations help us understand one another better. They keep us from labeling people with unkind terms like "odd" or "peculiar." They give us information about an individual. On the other hand, these designations can steer us away from remembering that each individual is a person created in God's image and is a full member of God's family.

This book, then, is an attempt to help churches remember. As we look at children and youth in our congregations who have been designated LD or AD/HD, these labels tell us that these individuals need some special handling in a typical classroom or worship setting. Perhaps it would help to associate the initials LD with "learning differences" as opposed to "learning disabilities." Keep in mind that we use initials and labels not to limit children but to acknowledge that we must be more creative and purposeful in our effort to educate and include all of God's children more effectively in our congregations.

As the title and subtitle of this book indicate, *Learning Disabilities and the Church* is intended to support the needs of all God's children, not just those who are known to have LD and AD/HD. The ideas and strategies outlined here will be helpful for many individuals. As someone who works with children and youth who have cognitive delays, emotional needs, and autism spectrum disorders, I'm convinced that the ideas in this book could support the learning environment for some of these individuals as well. Feel free to try some of these ideas with those who have other learning or medical designations. Consider this book a menu of choices—things to try. Every item will not work with every child, but by trying them you will develop a bank of strategies that help support the gifts and needs of each child in your congregation.

—Barbara J. Newman

INTRODUCTION

This book is written for you. It's for volunteer teachers and directors of Christian education; for Christian education committees and worship committees; for church boards, pastors, and other church staff who want to help children, young people, and families who are challenged with learning disabilities. Although our Presbyterian and Reformed perspective shapes this book, you'll find that much of the guidance offered will transfer to congregations from a variety of traditions and denominations. You'll also find that many of the strategies and ideas listed for individuals with LD and AD/HD transfer to support children with a wide variety of gifts and needs. Children with a cognitive delay, for example, may greatly benefit from the information in this book.

Our goal is to help readers find effective ways to accommodate and integrate into the life and ministry of congregations the many children, youth, and families who live with disabilities. Some families may join your church eagerly, having received great support and encouragement in the past. Others may join your congregation with some trepidation, having "failed" in the past to become part of a faith community that would accept them and their child with disabilities. There are times when kids with learning disabilities (LD) and Attention-Deficit/Hyperactivity Disorder (AD/HD) present behavior problems. They may have difficulty reading, writing, responding, listening, sitting still, and behaving appropriately in traditional worship and Sunday school settings. Such individuals can present a real challenge—and opportunity—for congregational ministries.

At least 4 million school-age children and youth in the United States are diagnosed with at least one form of learning disability (Medical College of Wisconsin Healthlink, http://healthlink.mcw.edu/article/1014733673.html). In Canada, government studies suggest that one in ten Canadians struggle with one or more learning disabilities—approximately 3 million Canadians (www.ldas.org/statistics.htm). These figures do not include those children and youth with mild or moderate disabilities who are not receiving special education services, nor does it include most children who are home-schooled, many of those who study in private schools and academies, and those with more moderate to severe disabilities. Given these numbers, it's likely that your congregation has already encountered one or more of the families described in this book. This book, then, is for you.

Jamie's Story

Jamie, a creative and imaginative child, had been described as "full of energy" and "all boy " since he was very small. In fact, his energy level seemed higher than that of the other kids in his preschool class—to the point that he was unable at times to participate constructively in class. Jamie often had difficulty paying attention and frequently disrupted class sessions. His parents, Bob and Sue, were encouraged to have Jamie evaluated for Attention-Deficit Hyperactivity Disorder (AD/HD). After testing Jamie, doctors concluded that Jamie's symptoms fit a diagnosis of AD/HD. They presented Bob and Sue with a variety of treatment options, both medication- and non-medication-based. In consultation with the doctors, Bob and Sue decided to try to manage Jamie's disorder through means other than medication.

But when Jamie entered public school, his behavior and learning issues grew more difficult. Jamie's behavior, heightened by the transition to a new school, new teacher, and new expectations, disrupted the class almost daily. Often Jamie reacted to this panoply of newness with anger and "inappropriate" behavior.

Soon after Jamie started first grade, the teachers and educational professionals met with Bob and Sue. They strongly recommended that Jamie be reevaluated for medication. Confronted with contradictory advice from professionals, friends, family, and the popular media, and with a growing sense of defeat and confusion, Bob and Sue decided to try medication. Thus began the years of trying to get the right medication and the right dosage for Jamie—all the while monitoring side effects and advocating for Jamie to receive the support he needed to succeed at school.

Bob and Sue often wondered whether they were making good choices. They wondered whether they were good parents, and whether Jamie would grow up to become a functioning and happy adult. Sometimes they disagreed with one another, which added stress to an already stressful home life. Despite educational testing that showed Jamie's high intelligence, the future often looked bleak.

When Jamie was small, his family had attended church regularly. They contributed financially and were active participants in a variety of ministries. Both Jamie and his younger sister had been baptized and welcomed into the faith community. Bob and Sue felt blessed by their participation in their church family.

But as Jamie grew into an "overactive" preschooler less able to sit quietly in worship and participate "appropriately" in Sunday school, several murmured complaints eventually got back to Bob and Sue. Jamie's church school teachers began to have difficulty with his behavior; ultimately fewer and fewer of them were willing to deal with him. They simply felt unqualified to deal with the challenges Jamie's presence brought to the class. The church's practice of rotating teachers from a team for each grade made matters worse. Jamie responded badly to each change of teacher, becoming aggressive in class. Other parents wanted to make sure Jamie would not be in their child's class. Comments like these began to filter up to the Sunday school and pastoral staff:

- "Either I can teach the lesson, or I can try to control Jamie."
- "We shouldn't be expected to try and handle him. His parents obviously can't handle him—anyway, it's their responsibility, not ours."
- "If I have to teach with him in the class, I quit."

Meanwhile, on a number of occasions the ushers encouraged the family to take Jamie out of the worship service because his behavior made it difficult for others to worship.

Eventually, Jamie's family decided to conserve their energy for dealing with the things that "really mattered"—Jamie's success at school. They dropped out of church. A few months later, the pastor called Bob and Sue to find out why they had left. The pastor made no mention of Jamie; in fact, he seemed completely in the dark about the issues their family was facing, and how the reaction of the church family to Jamie had hurt them. No one in the congregation seemed to care about what Bob and Sue were going through. They only seemed to care about making sure Jamie didn't bother them in worship or in Sunday school.

In the end, Bob and Sue concluded that, despite their own pain, it was all for the best. Sundays were a lot less hectic now, and the whole family had one day a week when they didn't have to struggle to make everything work.

What's Wrong with This Picture?

Sadly, families like Jamie's who are struggling with learning disabilities sometimes experience this lack of caring and understanding from their congregations. Parents like Bob and Sue face blame and shame as congregation members and staff express escalating irritation about the issues that children like Jamie raise in worship and Sunday school. No wonder dropping out of church seems like an acceptable solution to the "problem" of church participation.

It's clear that instead of blame and shame, what these families need is the care and compassion of a faith community.

Baptism: The Key to Our Role and Task

In the Reformed and Presbyterian tradition, congregations receive children into the faith community through baptism long before their skills, gifts, and abilities are known. They are baptized regardless of their skin color and before their personal likes and dislikes become evident. In baptism, the faith community acknowledges God's covenant promises and vows to nurture children and to support their parents and families as they grow in faith.

In addition to the baptismal promises made by parents and congregations at a child's baptism, Christians are called to follow Jesus and to welcome the stranger and the outcast, to care for those in need, and to proclaim Christ's good news to all. Our role is to let the children come to Jesus, and not to hinder them. Our task is clear: we must make the necessary accommodations to welcome those to whom we have a hard time extending Christian hospitality.

Thus, congregations have a responsibility to children and their families—regardless of whether or not they are challenged by learning disabilities. Congregations are called by God to become hospitable and safe places where children, youth, and families are accepted and valued, and where our common membership in Christ's body, the church, is celebrated. They are called to model the forming of disciples and to call all members to a life of service, witness, fellowship, and worship.

Children, youth, and families dealing with learning disabilities share in this calling to use the gifts and graces God has bestowed upon them for the service of all. As congregations consider the challenges, joys, and risks these members of God's family encounter on a daily basis, it becomes increasingly clear that their task is to develop effective methods that make possible the building of realistic and accessible paths for the establishment of identity as full members in the body of Christ—partners in God's movement of faith, witness, learning, service, and worship.

For parents of children and youth with learning disabilities, the demands are great and the stress can be high. Advocating for their children, educating themselves on options, working with teachers and mental health professionals, and striving to be "fair" to their other children can be very isolating for these parents. But as the body of Christ, we have family ties that are deeper and more authentic than those that are simply biological. We are all members of the family of God. So we reach out to assist the parents of children with special needs. And as we live out the baptismal covenant, we learn that parenting these children and welcoming them is a task shared by the entire community.

This book is written to assist congregations, through their education and worship communities, to become places of belonging for all God's children. Together we can learn to accommodate, to accept, to make room—and to celebrate!

What is at stake in the search for effective approaches to Christian education and worship ministries for children, youth, and families dealing with learning disabilities? This question points to a number of issues. Children with learning disabilities and their families are more likely to drop out of church than those who do not face such challenges, thus depriving congregations of their gifts and talents for years to come. These children can find school more challenging and they may be drawn into unhealthy activities ranging from asocial behavior to criminal activity. Their families might experience greater degrees of domestic conflict. The importance of ministering to this population is clear.

Overview

The following three chapters offer an overview of issues raised by the presence of children and youth with learning disabilities and their families in our faith communities.

- Using a series of frequently asked questions, chapter 1 describes the nature and substance of learning disabilities and Attention-Deficit/Hyperactivity Disorder and discusses issues for congregational ministry with children, youth, and their families who are challenged with these conditions.

- Chapter 2 deals with seven common learning and life differences in children and youth with learning disabilities and their families; it examines ways congregations can effectively minister to people with these particular issues.

- Chapter 3 points to how congregations can offer God's grace to these families through their education and worship ministries. It offers specific strategies for making accommodations to enable these children and youth to participate in church school and worship. And it challenges congregations to see a wider scope of possibilities for what it means to be the church—the body of Christ.

- Appendices include case stories with discussion questions about learning disability issues faced by congregations; a list of Scripture passages for preaching and teaching inclusion; ideas for celebrating inclusion in congregations; and a list of helpful organizations and websites. There's also an annotated bibliography for those who want to read more.

We offer this volume in the hope that through its use congregations may more fully reflect the light of Christ to a world that needs God's good news. God's rich blessings be upon you as you do this important work!

CHAPTER 1

Understanding Learning Disabilities (LD) and Attention-Deficit/Hyperactivity Disorder (AD/HD)

This chapter offers an overview of learning disabilities and Attention-Deficit/ Hyperactivity Disorder using a "frequently asked questions" format. It assumes little in the way of prior knowledge.

1. What are learning disabilities?

Learning disabilities, disorders, or differences (LD) are defined in a variety of ways. The more formal definitions that follow point to the fact that those with LD may not respond as desired or expected to traditional teaching methods. A Sunday school teacher, for example, might be telling a Bible story to a group that includes an individual who has an excellent vocabulary but who struggles to understand spoken words. When asked a question about the story, this child may have incomplete information. Individuals with learning differences, therefore, create opportunities for leaders to become more creative in their approach to teaching. Leaders must provide ways for each individual to connect with that Bible story—be that through words, pictures, songs, dramas, or wooden figures.

According to the National Institutes of Mental Health (NIMH), "LD is defined as a significant gap between a person's intelligence and the skills the person has achieved at each age."

In the U.S., the Individuals with Disability Education Act of 2004 (IDEA) defines learning disability as "a disorder in one or more of the basic psychological processes involved in understanding or in using spoken or written language, which may manifest itself in an imperfect ability to listen, think, speak, read, write, spell or to do mathematical calculations." This definition further states that learning disabilities include "such conditions as perceptual disabilities, brain injury, minimal brain dysfunction [and] dyslexia. . . ."

The Learning Disabilities Association of Canada defines learning disabilities as "a number of disorders which may affect the acquisition, organization, retention, understanding or use of verbal or nonverbal information. These disorders affect learning in individuals who otherwise demonstrate at least average abilities essential for thinking and/or reasoning. As such, learning disabilities are distinct from global intellectual deficiency."

Some researchers define LD as "a disorder that affects people's ability to either interpret what they see and hear or to link information from different parts of the brain." The dual issues of faulty *interpretation* and *linking* of information are key for our discussion.

Another condition that researchers and educational professionals do *not* consider a learning disability, while acknowledging its adverse impact on learning for many children and adults, is Attention-Deficit/Hyperactivity Disorder (AD/HD). Some symptoms of AD/HD include the following:

- over-activity or difficulty modulating activity level appropriate to an environment
- impulsivity—acting before thinking through consequences
- difficulties with sustained attention
- difficulty focusing, inability to concentrate, problems staying on task, persistent daydreaming
- poor organizational skills

Some people have the last two symptoms while showing few if any of the other symptoms. These individuals would be characterized as having Attention-Deficit/Hyperactivity Disorder—Predominantly Inattentive Type.

Since these conditions present similar challenges to congregational ministry, we address LD and AD/HD together.

Although the above list is a set of "symptoms," it's important to remember that along with these challenges often come gifts of creativity, vision, and energy. Many times an individual with AD/HD can see a solution to a problem that no one else can see. Focusing only on "symptoms" or "disabilities" often clouds our vision to see the possibilities and abilities in an individual.

As we consider individuals who have unique learning needs and present similar challenges to congregational ministry, we address LD and AD/HD together. Remember, however, that many children will benefit from a variety of teaching and response activities, not just those individuals with stated special needs.

2. Is it helpful or hurtful for an individual to be labeled as having LD or AD/HD?

In general, children receive these labels from a school assessment team, a psychologist, or a doctor. Although limited in their usefulness to capture a child's unique set of strengths and needs, designations can give information to others and help an individual get the services he or she may need to be successful in school or other environments. For example, if a person finds out that she has a hearing loss, she might want to use a hearing aid, a special amplification system for a classroom, and special seating in class. The designation of hearing loss allows a school system or insurance company to provide these services in response to the need. Without a diagnosis of hearing loss, that individual would not have access to support. The same is true for individuals with LD and AD/HD. Schools and other agencies can provide needed support for individuals with either designation. In that way, labels are helpful.

It can be hurtful, however, when others see only the label and not the person. People might make an assumption that because a child has AD/HD, the teacher in that classroom is in for a very bumpy ride. Making judgments based on a label can be hurtful. It's always important to get to know that child or youth as an individual. Dive into the pattern of gifts and needs tucked inside that gift to your community. Delight in opportunities to reach a growing mind. Use the label as a cue that you might need to make some changes or additions to adequately teach that individual, but count it as a joy.

3. Are people with LD or AD/HD cognitively impaired or developmentally delayed?

These conditions usually affect people of average or above-average intelligence, including some who might otherwise be labeled "gifted." It's also possible, for example, to have a child with Down Syndrome be diagnosed with a cognitive impairment as well as AD/HD. The combinations in children come in a wide variety, so it's important to know the individuals with whom you work, not just the letters behind the name. Although the focus of this book is on the vast majority of these individuals who are not cognitively impaired, many of the strategies could be helpful for a variety of people who have special needs.

4. Are LD and AD/HD real conditions or disorders?

There is some popular belief in the culture that LD and AD/HD are not real disorders—that if only parents and teachers were stricter, demanded more, or used adequate discipline, these disorders would fade from view. Another common religious misunderstanding is that if parents were simply more faithful, their children would be cured. Finally, some people of faith who accept that these disorders exist believe that prayer alone is the answer. These well-meaning Christians may blame parents and families for the very problems they are dealing with. Their attitudes are common enough that one evangelical Christian group has created a website to challenge them (www.christianadhd.com).

5. What behaviors do people with LD exhibit?

Although this is a list of some unique characteristics you might see in individuals with LD, remember that they describe only a small portion of what makes up an individual's unique learning profile. Where one individual might have needs in the area of understanding words, for example, her ability to build a complex Lego structure may be advanced far beyond her years. Use caution, therefore as you read this list:

- difficulty understanding and following instructions (you ask your class to look up a Bible passage, but Billy does not even move when the others start leafing through their books)

- trouble remembering what someone just told him or her (you just mentioned that the Christmas story is taken from Matthew and Luke, but Suzy asks a few minutes later where she should look to find the story)

- difficulty distinguishing right from left; difficulty identifying words; a tendency to reverse letters, words, or numbers (confusing 25 with 52, "b" with "d," or "on" with "no")

- difficulty reading or writing, sometimes to the point of refusing to engage in either activity

- saying words out loud while writing (a form of "self-accommodation" the child has developed in order to translate thoughts, which come more easily, into written communication, which is more difficult)

- seems to understand a concept one day but not the next

- shows a large gap between written ideas and understanding demonstrated through speech; expression and verbal understanding

You are probably asking yourself, "Don't most kids exhibit these behaviors?" The answer is yes, but usually not to such a degree that they consistently inhibit the child's ability to function or participate more fully in the group.

Only trained professionals can diagnose a condition of LD or AD/HD. You can, however, aid parents in getting help by bringing behaviors to their attention in a constructive manner. "Have you noticed that Suzy has trouble sitting still?" is appropriate; "Your little girl is obviously hyperactive" is not. You may be surprised to find out that Suzy has already been diagnosed but that her parents get tired of explaining why she is not "normal." In that case, "I've noticed Suzy has trouble sitting still. Can you give me some ideas about how to deal with this?" will get you a lot farther than, "How can I get your kid to stay in one place?"

6. What causes LD and AD/HD?

The medical world has made some amazing discoveries over the last few years. The availability of brain scans and well-funded research has created much discussion about the exact reason we see some of these differences in individuals. For those interested in understanding more about current research, the websites in Appendix D will be a great place to begin. For our purposes, however, understanding the cause is not nearly as important as understanding how we can best support those who have unique needs while utilizing their areas of strength. Suffice it to say, there is a growing sense that these conditions are "hard-wired" in the brain. The important thing to remember is that parents and families did not cause these conditions by traumatizing, mistreating, mismanaging, or neglecting their children. College educated parents are just as likely to have a child with one of these conditions as those with a high school diploma. Working mothers are no more likely to have a child with one of these conditions than those who stay home.

7. What is the scope of the problem?

Research suggests that at least 4 million school-age children in the United States have been diagnosed with LD. Of these, 20 percent have some kind of AD/HD that leaves them frequently unable to focus their attention. This means somewhere between 3 and 5 percent of U.S. schoolchildren have Attention-Deficit/Hyperactivity Disorder, the majority of whom are boys (Medical College of Wisconsin, http://healthlink.mcw.edu/article/1031002453.html). In Canada, government studies suggest that one in ten Canadians, approximately 3 million people, have one or more learning disabilities (www.cfc efc.ca/docs/ldac/00001132.htm; www.ldas.org/statistics.htm).

A few calculations will lead us to some reliable conclusions about the people in our pews on Sundays. If roughly 45 percent of the U.S. population of about 300 million (according to the 2000 census) identify themselves as Protestant Christians, between 4 million and 6.7 million Protestant Christians in the U.S. are likely to have diagnosable LD or AD/HD. That raises an interesting question: Just how many of these people are in church on a given Sunday? Demographers ask people about their religious self-identification, knowing that many will name a particular tradition without implying active participation in a local congregation of any type. How many of the people in that 4 to 7 million have found some congregation, any congregation, to be a safe space where they can invest in the life and ministry of that faith community? How many have felt themselves excluded, or have excluded themselves, because of their unwillingness to risk not fitting in in yet another context? This is a crucial question for us and for our ministry.

8. What are the different forms of LD?

Learning disabilities can be divided into many categories. Psychologists have codes and numbers to very specifically define the type of need in each child. Although important educationally, it might be most helpful to talk about general categories. Some researchers divide LDs into these three broad categories:

- *Developmental speech and language disorders,* in which children have difficulty producing speech sounds, using spoken language to communicate, or understanding what other people say. Because of the primacy of the development of speech in order to communicate and respond, this kind of LD is often identified earlier in life than the other two. Additionally, this is the most commonly identified and diagnosed of the three forms of LD, with 85-90 percent of school-aged children diagnosed with LD manifesting specific reading or language-based disabilities.

- *Academic skill disorders,* in which children have difficulty with the development of the skills needed to read, write, or do arithmetic. These are often diagnosed in the early years of a child's schooling.

- *"Other" disorders.* This catch-all category includes certain coordination disorders and learning handicaps not covered by the other terms. These may include motor skills disorders and other diagnoses that do not meet the criteria of a specific learning disability included in the first two categories.

In addition, although they are not considered true learning disabilities, the prevalence of a fourth category deserves our attention here.

- *Attention-Deficit/Hyperactivity Disorder,* in which children seem to daydream excessively, are easily distracted, and tend to mentally drift. Teachers and parents often report of children with attention concerns that they "seem to be in a world of their own." Attention-Deficit/Hyperactivity Disorder suggests three categories or types: Predominantly Inattentive Type, Predominantly Hyperactive-Impulsive Type, and Combined Type. Because of the "quiet" nature of symptoms in attention deficit without hyperactivity, some children with Attention-Deficit/Hyperactivity Disorder—Predominantly Inattentive Type are much less likely to receive diagnosis early, and may drift academically for some years before receiving assistance.

9. What kinds of educational and medical professionals work with children who have LD and AD/HD?

Parents of children and youth with these types of special needs often find themselves working with a wide range of education, medical, and other professionals as they seek to help their child. The sheer number of people with whom they deal in a given week can be overwhelming. This situation makes it essential for the church to be pastoral in its ministry rather than clinical.

10. What are the legal issues?

United States citizens with LD and AD/HD have a variety of legal rights under the Americans with Disabilities Act and other acts. Canadian citizens with LD and AD/HD are protected through the Canadian Human Rights Act, which is multifaceted legislation that seeks to address the rights of persons made legally vulnerable by a variety of conditions and circumstances. As private institutions, churches are exempt from these laws. However, you may have occasion to advise parishioners who feel their rights are not being protected or who may not even be aware of them. If the individual is school age, parents may appreciate the support of having a friend from church attend meetings. That could allow the parent to focus on the needs of the child, while the accompanying friend can focus on obtaining the best support possible for the child and on understanding the laws of protection. Tapping into the expertise of school staff and working with them as a team is often the best way to understand what kind of support is available. In some cases, the best course of action is to refer people to a qualified attorney. For the purposes of congregational ministry, knowing about these laws can help us in our work with children, youth, and families.

Knowing that an LD diagnosis itself can lead to a negative understanding of the child by teachers and other adults, congregations can model acceptance of all people and their gifts and, as Paul reminds us, work to see people as Christ would see them, and not from a human point of view (2 Cor. 5:16).

Even though individuals with special needs have certain protection under the law, churches have an opportunity to deal with people under the law of love. Imagine being included or served because the law requires it, in contrast with having someone make special arrangements for you because they *want* to include you. What an amazing message of inclusion, understanding, and honor the latter would communicate to a fellow brother or sister in Christ! Our basis for inclusion in a church, therefore, is not first of all obedience to the laws of the land but obedience to the way God wants us to live as his body.

11. How do schools approach children who have been diagnosed with LD?

Public schools and other publicly funded institutions serving elementary, middle school, and high school students follow a rather standard set of steps once a child has been diagnosed with LD.

When a diagnosis has been reached, an individualized education program (IEP) will be formed. The IEP will outline in detail every accommodation that the school, in consultation with the parents or guardians, sees as appropriate to both the diagnosis and to the collective experience of all adults involved with the child. These accommodations can range from strategic seating, to time out of class with a special education support staff to work individually or with a small group on assignments that are particularly difficult for a student, to the development of different ways for the student's progress to be assessed.

An IEP is also important for a youth taking standardized college entrance exams such as SAT and ACT. Many teens with special needs will benefit from college and university special education programs. Such assistance can make all the difference in achieving academic success and receiving a college diploma.

As a pastor or Sunday school teacher, you will not have access to the child's IEP unless parents choose to share it with you. Bear in mind that a few parents may not be happy with the IEP, and that they may feel that the school is doing less than it should to accommodate a student's needs. Even if the IEP is perfect, parents may be reluctant to share it. Again, a pastoral rather than a clinical approach may elicit the cooperation you need. "Tell me, how does Joan learn best?" will help establish trust and build relationships with the family.

12. What about medications?

The use of medications for treating children and youth with LD and AD/HD is controversial. Comments such as, "We're drugging our kids too much" or "Don't you worry about putting your kids on drugs?" add to parents' already considerable load of guilt. You need not know—nor is it appropriate to ask—if a child is medicated unless his safety depends on such knowledge. For example, medical release forms used for youth trips should list any medications the child takes. These forms should be held in the strictest confidence and revealed to chaperones and other volunteers on a strictly need-to-know basis.

The decision to medicate a child is a difficult one that parents should make only in consultation with a qualified physician. Under routine circumstances, it is seldom appropriate for church staff to discuss options about medication with parents, and it is *never* appropriate to suggest that a child be medicated. Only a doctor should do that.

13. How does the presence of a child or youth with LD or AD/HD in a household impact the rest of the family?

The condition of one member affects everyone in the family. Children with LD or AD/HD may realize that they are different from other children their age. Some will not understand why they are behind in school or what makes them different. Others may have participated in activities and evaluations that allow them to better understand their learning profile. Many of these children have had the chance to see how the strengths they have can help support the challenges. At times, children with special needs in one area may also have a very high level of intelligence. Most of the time considered a positive quality, their above-average intelligence can add to their frustration. Many times, children with learning challenges may have those "head" concerns (issues related to learning information) lead into places of "heart" concerns (issues related to emotions and self-concept.).

Without proper intervention, some come to know that their differences are keeping them from conforming to "age-appropriate" expectations. This awareness can lead to embarrassment and low self-esteem.

In other cases, these negative feelings can cause children and youth with LD or AD/HD to "act out" in ways that affect the whole family. Acting out may take the form of withdrawal or of belligerence. It is not uncommon for these children to get into fights with peers. Fights in the home with siblings and/or parents can become common as well. Finally, some of these children also struggle with depression. It's critical that children receive many opportunities to understand that every individual is a unique package of gifts and needs. Understanding their own gifts and needs can free children to maintain a strong and positive "heart" despite their struggles with the "mind" required during the school years.

Having a child with LD or AD/HD can be an emotional challenge for the entire family. Parents may experience guilt, frustration, anger, or despair. Brothers and sisters may become irritated at the amount of attention this "special" child receives, particularly if the "normal" children are doing well in school and at home. Congregations need to be aware of the potential stress experienced by these families and seek ways to minister with all members in appropriate, effective, and relevant ways.

It's important for families and church families to understand that the issues related to LD and AD/HD are often the most difficult during the school years. School and educational settings require a huge amount of attention skills and learning ability—especially learning that relates to language understanding and usage. Once they have come through the school years, these individuals can choose a profession that will best suit their gifts and needs. So you'll want to help families see beyond these times that sometimes seem filled with struggles. That child may one day become the elder who is able to see a solution to a church issue no one else was able to see. That young person may become the most creative Sunday school teacher on your staff. Stress the uniqueness of these children of God as you do all others. Avoid reporting every little classroom issue to parents. Emphasize the contributions they make to church activities. Do not make their families feel that their children are a burden requiring too much energy from staff and volunteers.

CHAPTER 2

Common Differences
in Children and Youth
with LD and AD/HD

This chapter outlines some of the most common differences in children and youth with learning disabilities that affect congregational ministry. Understanding the particular areas of need faced by these children and families will help you effectively shape your ministry with them in an informed and relevant way. Remember that differences can lead to areas of need, but they can also lead to areas of blessing in an individual's life. Also remember that no two children are exactly alike. These areas, then, can only be a set of general guidelines as you seek to understand each individual God has brought to your group or area of ministry. You'll find specific strategies to address these common areas in chapter 3.

1. Learning in Different Ways
Enlightened educators sometimes say that the minds of children and youth with LD and AD/HD work in interesting—and unexpected—ways. At any given time, these children and youth may be thinking not about the task or subject at hand, but rather about a subject that was addressed earlier in the class—or earlier in the year. Or they could be considering an angle of the subject under discussion that no one else in the class—student or teacher—has ever explored.

Because many children and youth with LD are quite intelligent, it should not surprise us when their insights (which may seem to come out of left field) are striking and remarkably in-depth. At other times their comments will seem entirely off base. Teachers often try to suppress these "inappropriate" responses because they need to "get on with the lesson."

Like all of us, each of these children has a preferred learning style. Some kids with LD and AD/HD need something tangible to work with—paper, clay, or crayons. Others find their strength in verbal interplay and are greatly troubled by a requirement of silence. Some enjoy artistic expression, reveling in music, art, and dance. Others seem to need the whole room—or the whole church building—in which to roam during their time with you. Still others prefer small spaces, choosing to sit under a table or in a corner in order to block out distractions. Many children and youth with LD and AD/HD have a great gift of imagination; others, for whom abstract thinking is difficult, will not participate in an activity that calls for imaginative thinking. And some have lots of imagination but struggle with the inability to discern the difference between fact and fantasy. Some of these children and youth read well silently but cannot read aloud; others can read only out loud but cannot do so silently, while still others hardly read at all. Some write creative and wonderful stories; others can hardly write a word and become very distressed when expected to do so. What can make these children so challenging is not that they have a preferred learning style, but that they do not easily move out of their preferred style into other ways of learning.

Those of us who have been blessed with so-called "typical" ways of approaching the world (as defined by the majority) must remember how often these children receive the message that they can't "fit in," no matter how hard they try. The more we strive to bridge the gaps in our own understanding, the better our ministries will be, both for those who lead in worship and Sunday school and for our members who struggle with LD.

Some curriculums for Sunday school and youth groups now better understand that each person comes with unique gifts and needs. Faith Alive (publisher of this book), for example, publishes curricula (*Walk With Me; Kid Connection*) based on the theory of multiple intelligences. Each lesson approaches the class with movement, speaking, songs, games, art, and more. Although leaders can be creative in adapting material, it's worthwhile to begin with curriculum that already understands that we all learn in different ways.

2. Transition Issues

Most children have difficulty transitioning from one activity or task to another. For children and youth with LD and AD/HD, however, transitions are especially difficult. Seemingly simple moves from one kind of activity to another—from one space in the classroom to another; from working alone to working with a group; from education to fellowship and from fellowship to worship—prove exceptionally challenging. The potential anxiety caused by transition may force these children into "shut-down mode"—a refusal to make the transition at all. Others, particularly those who are younger, may cry or respond with other inappropriate behaviors. Older children and youth, particularly those at or beyond adolescence, may move with the group but mentally "check out" for the next activity.

The good news is that there are ways we can assist these children and youth in developing greater ability to make transitions in healthy ways. Because transitions are an inescapable fact of life, it is important for us to find ways to increase the children's comfort level with change and transitions in worship and Sunday school. Because transition issues do impact a large group of children, not only those identified as having special needs, addressing this issue will help support a large number of children in your group.

3. Focus Issues

Many children and youth with LD and AD/HD find it difficult to focus on one thing at a time or to choose the most important thing on which to focus. These children often seem to "space out" or daydream through class; they never seem to be fully present for any activity. Being called back into the present with comments such as "Hello" or "Are you with us?" or "Pay attention" may serve to embarrass the student but does not produce any lasting results (except perhaps to make the student even more withdrawn).

Focus issues can be caused by a wide variety of factors: imbalances in brain chemistry; prenatal brain injury; problems with processing information received, either visually or aurally; problems with understanding the body language of others; various disorders of the central nervous system; or stress and anxiety stemming from a host of issues that make life a struggle for these children and youth.

Coupled with these factors are some aspects of the physical space itself. The way the room is arranged, the colors in the space (flooring, walls, ceiling), the variety of textures used in the room, the pictures on the wall, the way people are dressed, noises inside or outside the building—all of these can impact the child with a learning disability in his or her effort to focus. In addition, as we have noted before, if there are changes in the space from week to week, many children with learning disabilities will still be adjusting to these changes when others have already begun worship or learning. This is particularly the case when there are regular monthly changes of teaching staff in worship or Sunday school, a common practice in many congregations. So individuals with LD are always playing a game of catch-up—a game that, as they have learned through painful experience, they will inevitably lose. Because paying attention and learning require more effort from children and youth with LD and AD/HD, they are likely to tire and to do so more quickly than their peers without learning disabilities.

Another issue that is particularly confusing to many observers of LD behavior is the ability many of these children and youth have to "hyper-attend." They may be so absorbed in a particular activity that nothing can pry them away from it. This hyper-attention can go on for an incredibly long time, which can become quite frustrating to the parent, teacher, or worship leader. They may find themselves asking, "Why can't this child be respectful of me and everyone else by following my lesson?"

The problem for many children and youth with LD and AD/HD is that their minds seem to constantly operate at high speed, racing like an out-of-control car from one place to another. Such children often lose patience with the slow pace of one activity and want to move to the next. Failing this, the mind finds its own recourse by immersing the child in his or her own thoughts. This tendency to hyper-focus can result in intense bursts of creativity when properly channeled. It can also lead to a desire for distraction, which explains the fascination these young people often have with video games. These games provide the intense stimulation and rapidly changing challenges people with LD and AD/HD often crave.

The ability to hyper-attend can be a gift of grace to children or youth with LD or AD/HD and their families, if adults can discern ways to direct that ability in ways that are useful to society. Many children and youth with LD or AD/HD are particularly gifted with hyper-attention and rapid thinking skills, which are greatly valued in adulthood in some work places. Additionally, people who have a knack for thinking quickly and hyper-attending can be a great gift for the ministry of a congregation. Beginning to see these "negative" abilities in a positive light can be the beginning of transforming a congregation.

4. Structure and Routine

Because children and youth with LD and AD/HD have problems with focus and making transitions, they have a greater need for structure than their peers. While these young people may not appreciate structure, providing it allows them to concentrate their energies on handling the task at hand rather than on managing their environment. Making life predictable can greatly aid these children and youth.

Unfortunately, much of life is not predictable. Relatives and friends come to visit; school and congregation evening and weekend programs change; holidays roll around with regularity—all of which sends the regular family schedule out the window.

In the Sunday school classroom and in worship, routine is often lacking for one reason or another. Creative teaching, which is to be encouraged, often implies some spontaneity, which can be disconcerting for a child with LD or AD/HD. A teacher may, on a sunny day, decide to hold class outside, upsetting the class routine. Many congregations use rotating groups of teachers and worship leaders, which further undermines consistency. In non-liturgical, "free church" worship styles, the pace and substance of worship and education leadership can vary greatly from week to week.

Recognizing that certain children and youth really do require high structure, adult consistency, and clear expectations has implications for our ministry. For some people, the good news is best delivered in consistent and constant classroom and worship settings. Discerning ways to effectively and creatively integrate these aspects and needs into our ministries is a priority.

5. Impulsivity and Lack of Maturity

Many children and youth with LD or AD/HD are perceived as behaving in ways that are not "age-appropriate." Because standard developmental theory dictates that all children reach specific milestones at a certain point, we expect kids to demonstrate "age-appropriate" behavior.

Children and youth with LD or AD/HD often act impulsively in ways we expect of younger children. Their impulse control is impaired, and it develops later than it does for their peers. In Sunday school classrooms and in worship, this lack of maturity and impulse control can be challenging. Behaviors such as an inability to wait one's turn; speaking out before being called upon; being loud when silence is expected; inability to sit still; and impatience with the pace of activities may all interfere with normal activities.

Ironically, a teacher's efforts to control inappropriate behavior may exacerbate the problem. Punishing children for behavior they cannot control will be counterproductive. While we may be tempted to encourage a child or youth who doesn't want to be "treated like a baby" to "stop acting like one!" such an approach will almost certainly not achieve the goals of gaining a child's trust, nor of engaging the child more fully with the rest of the group, nor of doing ministry in the name of Jesus. Addressing the lack of impulse control in a sensitive manner that allows both the child or youth and others present to avoid embarrassment and to continue to feel a sense of belonging to the group is not easy. But discerning and remaining focused on the goal of our ministry with children, youth, and families can assist us in finding ways to approach people that are faithful, just, and that engender peace and depth in our relationships in Christ.

6. Self-Esteem

Healthy self-esteem is vital to the well-being of all people. Everyone has experienced the erosion of self-esteem that comes at moments of vulnerability. For most of us these episodes are brief, and we have the emotional reserves to recover. Our successes exceed our failures, the love of family and friends sustains us, and the church constantly reminds us of our inherent worth and God's unconditional love for us.

But for children and youth with LD and AD/HD, the experience of lowered self-esteem can be life-long if not properly addressed during childhood.

Researchers have discovered that as early as third grade, these children see themselves as less capable than their peers. School can be particularly harmful for their self-esteem. Schools and educational settings can also be supportive and create a life-long positive framework in which that child can operate.

Continual exposure to academic struggle and failure has been shown to lead to a reaction of "learned helplessness" in many children and youth with LD or AD/HD. Experience reinforces the notion that they will never be able to control their situation and encourages these students to avoid new tasks altogether: "I'll fail anyway," they reason, "so why even try?" On the other hand, experiences that are designed to tap into each person's gift areas and compensate for areas of need can give all children a sense of belonging and reward for personal contributions. How schools, churches, and families are set up will make a huge positive or negative impact on the life of each child.

The self-esteem of children and youth with LD or AD/HD is a complex issue. Research done by Dr. Margaret D. Clark at California State University suggests that teachers unwittingly contribute to the problem of poor self-esteem. Knowing that a child is LD and/or AD/HD, teachers often assume limited ability and lower their expectations for that child. Even when he or she does well, teachers may fail to offer the praise and encouragement they routinely give to students without learning disabilities. It's important, therefore, to understand each child's unique gifts and needs. Have the expectation that each person needs to contribute to the group in order to be fully functional. "Each one should use whatever gift he has received . . ." (1 Pet. 4:10). Make that a group standard, and delight in each contribution.

Finally, we need to note the relationship of stress and self-esteem. Weakened self-esteem creates stress; and stress in turn makes us vulnerable to further erosions of confidence. Children and youth with LD or AD/HD experience stress at a higher level and more often than their peers. Stress leads to fatigue, which renders kids even less able to cope with challenging situations. Reflecting on what we can do to help relieve stress for children and youth with LD or AD/HD and their families can lead us to effective and helpful ministry initiatives.

7. Learning Disabled . . . and Gifted

You have probably never seen these terms connected. Indeed, many educators consider them mutually exclusive. How can a child have learning disabilities and also be gifted? Hard as it may be to accept, many individuals with LD or AD/HD are "gifted." They are sometimes referred to as having "dual exceptionalities" (see www.kidsource.com/education/dual.exception.html). The tendency of educators to dismiss these young people as having low ability causes them to overlook many of the special gifts and talents these individuals possess. Funding constraints also make it difficult to nurture children's unique abilities while addressing their learning disabilities. Forced to choose between programs, educators opt to remediate rather than challenge.

Researchers have identified three categories among children and youth who are gifted and have learning disabilities:

- *Students identified as gifted with subtle learning disabilities.* These students often exhibit a marked discrepancy between expected and actual performance. They have been identified as extremely bright, and so the expectation level of schools and parents is high. But because of their often undiagnosed learning disabilities, they struggle to perform as expected. When they fail to receive assistance with their specific learning challenges, these children and youth are at risk of falling behind their peers and not being able to play to their obvious strengths as the work of keeping up with others takes an increasing amount of time and effort as they grow older.

- *Unidentified students.* These students have not been tested either for learning disabilities or giftedness; often because their strengths compensate for their learning challenges in such a way that they are able to keep up with the curriculum. In a twist on the adage "the squeaky wheel gets the grease," these students often struggle quietly. In the words of researcher Susan Baum, "their gift masks the disability and the disability masks the gift" (www.kidsource.com/kidsource/content/Gifted_learning_disabled.html). These students don't know that they are gifted, nor do they know that they have LD and/or AD/HD. In most cases they identify themselves as average students.

- *Students who are identified as having learning disabilities who are also gifted.* These children and youth often struggle the most at school. They are generally noticed first because of what they *cannot* do rather than because of the incredible talent that they demonstrate in some area. These students are at significant risk because of the ways educators understand a diagnosis of LD, and how they apply that diagnosis. It's really important, therefore, to have evaluators who see both the gifts and needs of each child. These people can not only encourage children to use their gifts, but can suggest specific ways to use those gifts to support their areas of need.

These groups of children and youth are often acutely aware of the ways in which they cannot perform on the same level as their peers, leading some of them to act out their frustration in Sunday school or worship settings. Worship leaders and teachers need to develop compensatory strategies for these children and youth to make it easier for them to demonstrate their gifts to themselves and others. The church has a mandate to value differences as we engage with these children and youth in our ministries.

In this chapter, we have outlined seven areas of difference in children and youth with LD and AD/HD and their families. These issues occur regularly in the lives of these children and youth at school, at home, and in their life in the community—including in the congregation. In the next chapter, we discuss ways to develop effective and relevant ministry with these children, youth, and their families, through the grace of accommodation.

CHAPTER 3

Ministering to Children and Youth with LD and AD/HD

Theologian and author Brett Webb-Mitchell notes that "Christian religious education with people with disabilities . . . is going to be more complicated . . . because the theories of Christian religious education have been constructed, in large part, *without people with disabling conditions in mind*" (*Unexpected Guests at God's Banquet: Welcoming People with Disabilities into the Church*, p. 134). This oversight applies to many Sunday school curricula and to the assumptions held by many Sunday school teachers and worship leaders.

Our job is more complicated when we become serious about including all whom God has welcomed. But it is not impossible. By God's grace, we continue to learn effective strategies to welcome and make room for all God's children, including those with disabilities. This is good news for children and youth with learning disabilities and for their families.

In many congregations, though, welcome is not extended and adequate room is not found for children and youth with LD and AD/HD. Activating strategies of accommodation in order to make our worship spaces and Sunday school programs safe and welcoming places for the vulnerable in our midst requires us *to act*.

This chapter suggests many ways that we can develop strategies, with the grace of God, to welcome children and youth with LD and AD/HD and their families to join the congregation in ministry, witness, and service. Remember that the following ideas can also be effective for many different children—not only those designated as having LD or AD/HD. Some of these strategies are quite simple and can be activated in the classroom or worship service without a lot of planning and consultation. We offer some relatively simple first steps you can use as an interim strategy to begin to make changes. These steps can offer an authentic beginning for your congregation to open the doors wider and become more deeply hospitable to anyone who enters.

Other strategies call for more time, more planning, more consultation, and perhaps more consciousness-raising than any one person in your congregation can accomplish. These are the steps that you'll need to pray about, to discuss, and to explore with others. Moving your congregation to make an investment and commitment to welcoming all God's children will take time, energy, and leadership. As you begin this process of discerning the ways God is calling your congregation to this important ministry, remember that the Spirit of God has already broken the path. May knowing that you go this way at God's invitation, and that you go *with* God, strengthen you for the journey.

The First Step: Making Accommodations
The first step in making accommodations for children and youth who learn in different ways is to acknowledge that *they are already in our Christian education classrooms and worship spaces.* Acknowledging this fact increases our awareness of the urgency of offering effective accommodations for everyone's sake. The following strategies for accommodation form the foundation of an overall approach of faithful hospitality and welcome for all your congregation's ministries.

Some public and private school accommodations can be applied to congregational ministries as well. According to Barbara Newman, a Christian educator and advocate for kids with disabilities, "God can use what we have learned in the classroom setting to help congregations better enfold children" (*Helping Kids Include Kids with Disabilities*, p. 7). The recommendations on these pages are based on the work of a number of experts in the field, especially on Grad Flick's helpful book *How to Reach and Teach Teenagers with ADHD.* Although Flick's work is aimed at a particular learning challenge—AD/HD—and a particular age group—teens—many of the accommodations suggested here can help children and youth of a variety of ages who are dealing with a wide variety of learning challenges.

This chapter recommends strategies for accommodation in four areas:

- *Accommodations for teachers and worship leaders.* Changing teachers' attitudes and the way they teach and lead can make a big difference for children and youth with LD and AD/HD, and their families, increasing their chance to participate successfully in Sunday school and worship.

- *Accommodations in the setting.* These strategies have to do with physical space, furnishings, and tools.

- *Accommodations children and youth with LD and AD/HD can make for themselves.* These strategies can be a real boost to children's self-esteem.

- *Accommodations families can reinforce at home.* Most Sunday school teachers and worship leaders know the increased faith development that takes place in kids when parents and guardians reinforce the learning that happens at church in their homes. Learning, worship, and faith development that takes place in the home is a significant part of a holistic approach to all ministries.

Accommodations may be initiated and reinforced by more than one person or group involved in your education and worship ministries. Teachers and worship leaders, children and youth, and parents and guardians all have a role to play in carrying out strategies of accommodation. And all of these accommodations must be acknowledged (and sometimes approved by) the church's governing leaders. This is another step toward a holistic church-wide approach to accommodation and welcome of all into the family of God.

Accommodations for Teachers and Worship Leaders

The accommodations discussed in this section are neither difficult, costly, nor time-consuming to implement. Most congregations can implement them with the staff and resources currently available. They do, however, require some additional consciousness-raising, training, and planning. You can incorporate such preparation into staff meetings, workshops, teacher training sessions, or other suitable formats. Advance planning and information sharing are crucial, and so is developing a comprehensive plan to incorporate all children into the life of the church. Such a plan ought to address the following questions:

- What is our main goal in education ministry?

- What is our main goal in education ministry with children and youth with LD and AD/HD, and their families?

- What is our main goal in worship ministry?

- What is our main goal in worship ministry with children and youth with LD and AD/HD, and their families?

- Where do these goals overlap? Do any of our overall ministry goals in education and worship change because of this awareness?

- In order for our congregation to achieve these goals,

    what steps will be required?

    who needs to take part?

    what meetings will need to be held?

what resources are needed?

what new or expanded programming do we foresee?

- Do we need increased staff, paid or volunteer? Barbara Newman (*Helping Kids Include Kids with Disabilities,* pp. 17-18) encourages congregations to consider adding the position of a coordinator for children with special needs to your staff. How will your congregation increase its ministry for this special population, and what roles would an additional person or persons play?

- In smaller churches that may not be in a position to add staff persons, different strategic questions arise, including the following:

  Who in our congregation has expertise and training in working with children and youth who have learning disabilities?

  Who might be willing and able to be trained as an adult friend for children and youth who have learning disabilities?

  Which other congregations can potentially partner with us to offer ministry to children and youth who have learning disabilities, and their families?

- What kind of training do we need? Who needs to receive training? Who will do the training?

- What special skills do church members and staff possess that will add to this new ministry?

- How will we assess the effectiveness of our ministry to children and youth with LD and AD/HD, and their families?

As you read through the following suggestions, remember that you'll want to adapt them to your own unique congregation and situation.

- **Increase your knowledge.** Reading this book is a good place to start. The resources listed in the Bibliography will guide you through further reading.

- **Involve parents and families.** Meet with parents and ask for their advice about what works for their child and what creates more difficulties. Like all parents, they have goals for their children. This simple act is grace-filled; you may be the first person representing the church who has cared enough to inquire.

  Remember that parents of children and youth with LD and AD/HD could be stressed, frustrated, and exhausted. Some may have painful histories of being confused and rejected as they sought to learn about their child. They fear that they and their child will be rejected or judged harshly. Work, then, to earn and receive their trust. Work confidentially with shared information. And work to make education and worship ministry a positive experience for their family, as you do for the families of all the children and youth in your care.

- **Develop a plan.** Making accommodations specific to the needs of a particular child requires planning. In developing this plan, strive to be pastoral rather than clinical. Talk with the parents, observe the child, and decide on appropriate adjustments. You may wish to invite the parents to the classroom for several sessions. Does the child need a faith partner? Can the child arrive early so that he or she can greet the other children as they arrive and the group forms around them as the initial activity gets underway? Try several strategies and review them as the year progresses. (For more on involving parents in developing a plan, see *Helping Kids Include Kids with Disabilities.*)

- **Model acceptance.** Children and youth in your class and in your worship services learn from every move, word, and gesture you make. They learn from what you do and from what you don't do. Remembering that children and youth with LD and AD/HD approach worship and Sunday school differently than their peers can help us focus on the need to model our acceptance and valuing of difference. God made each of us unique, and our uniqueness is part of God's plan. Those who learn differently have frequent moments of insight that might not occur to others. So we need to create safe places where such insights can be shared. We need to celebrate our differences.

- **Be flexible.** Adjusting your expectations of what can and will take place gives everyone a better chance to achieve the goals of the lesson or to participate meaningfully in worship.

- **Take your time.** The presence of children or youth with LD and AD/HD in your class may mean you will not always finish your lesson plan. Take your time—it will reduce your agenda anxiety and your students' stress—and increase everyone's opportunity to have a positive experience.

- **Give advance notice of transitions.** Write your schedule on the board or make a schedule using pictures. Review it before you begin. Then be disciplined about telling participants when a transition is approaching: "Five minutes until clean-up time."

- **Build relationships.** Many children and youth with LD and AD/HD don't easily trust a new person. Patience, consistency, clear expectations, kindness, interest, and time can help you form a relationship with a child who has particular difficulty in relating to others. If your congregation rotates teachers and worship leaders, be sure to introduce the next teacher to the child and parents a week ahead of the change.

- **Provide structure and routine.** As noted in chapter 2, this is a crucial need for children and youth with LD and AD/HD. A consistent routine helps everyone in knowing what to expect and what is expected of them. Keep the classroom routines the same, and provide variation within each activity. Alert the family ahead of time when the schedule will be different for combined classes, Christmas program rehearsals, or other special events. Together the family and child can decide whether or not to participate or wait until the regular routine resumes.

  This accommodation is made simpler because many Sunday school curricula offer a standard pattern of steps that occur in every lesson. The addition of a ritual or pattern can start with that which is already built into the curriculum.

- **Establish ritual.** The Christian tradition has a rich tradition of liturgical ritual that can be used positively with children and youth with LD and AD/HD. Repetition of songs, symbols, gestures, and use of tangible objects—candles, stoles, banners—helps engage everyone in ministry. Using worship ritual can help build impulse control skills over time, with the result that impulsive behavior decreases. In worship, children learn to anticipate what will happen next and how they can participate in the liturgy.

  Ritual can be used in the Sunday school classroom as well. Your church's curriculum, worship style, context, and ministry will determine what particular rituals make sense and work best for your students. Teachers and all students will benefit from sticking to the same routines so everyone knows what to expect.

- **Explore options for worship leadership.** As we noted in chapter 2, a number of children and youth with LD and AD/HD are gifted in one or more areas. Seek out opportunities for everyone in your group to lead worship in some way. Options for such leadership include reading Scripture, playing an instrument or singing, writing prayers or poems for worship, or creating artwork that can be used as banners, posters, or bulletin art. Discerning the gifts among the children and youth with whom you serve makes it possible for them to offer these gifts to the whole congregation in ministry.

- **Reduce the number of transitions.** Worship leaders and teachers need to review their lesson plan and see how many changes in activity, mode, and venue they can reduce. Remember that establishing a worship ritual that maintains a similar structure for every session makes transitions easier. If possible, have all students attend a singing time before going into their class groupings in order to avoid interrupting class times with an outside activity. Kids will be most comfortable when they learn to expect what is coming next.

- **Prepare children and youth for upcoming changes** in the routine. Inform students of changes early on and often so that everyone has a chance to prepare both internally and externally. This is vital for success in regular weekly classes; it is even more so for unusual events like pageants, Easter programs, all-church gatherings, musicals, and the like that may be part of your education and worship ministry. You'll also want to alert the families of children and youth with LD and AD/HD so they can plan and work with leaders to help their child participate successfully in the activity.

- **Integrate exercise and movement** into your regular classroom or worship routine. Stretching and movement helps reduce stress and increases everyone's ability to focus. Movement can also be used as a reward when an assignment is finished. Listen to the day's Scripture while standing up. Allow children to choose whether they prefer to work sitting or standing at a table.

- **Avoid information overload.** Be prepared to cover less material, if need be. The curriculum your congregation uses may suggest covering more material than some students can integrate in a session. As worship leaders and classroom teachers get to know students, they may need to work with pastoral staff and Christian education committees to adjust their expectations about how much material is covered in a particular class. Adapting expectations to fit the needs of those in the class will give everyone in the class a more positive experience of learning and growth. Remember to provide information in a variety of ways, using as many senses as possible.

- **Establish priorities about behavior.** Create a list of acceptable behaviors and work with Christian education leaders to develop and post a "contract" of behavior for the class. This might include such behaviors as raising a hand before speaking, showing respect for others, and following directions. The contract should also outline consequences for unacceptable behaviors (see below). You may want to send a copy of the contract home with each child to be signed by children and their families.

  Remember that sensitive teachers and worship leaders will tolerate minor over-activity as a way to accommodate kids with LD and AD/HD.

- **Provide consequences for inappropriate behavior.** When inappropriate behavior occurs repeatedly in the classroom, teachers should seek help from trained Christian education leaders or worship staff. These leaders will need to verify that the child did understand posted classroom rules, as consequences for actions that result from a child's confusion about appropriate behavior are not effective in changing the behavior over time. Remember that consequences inform a child *what not to do;* they do not teach *what to do.*

Teachers and leaders should work together to develop a consistent plan for how they will respond to repeated inappropriate behavior. Such a plan should specify acceptable consequences and at what point they are implemented. These consequences should be part of the contract establishing classroom standards of behavior. The contract needs to be reviewed and understood by all children, parents, teachers, and staff at the beginning of each new Sunday school season.

Involve families of kids with LD and AD/HD at the start of each year in helping teachers identify how to work with their children. Discuss how families will be involved with teachers and staff in dealing with inappropriate behaviors. Remember that removing the child entirely from the class or program attendance will only alienate the family and is not an appropriate solution.

- **Redirect inappropriate behavior.** This is a common technique for ending misbehavior in all grade and ability levels. The teacher or worship leader distracts the child or youth by verbally redirecting him or her with a question, by commenting on new lesson facts, or by changing the current activity when problems begin to occur.

- **Review rules frequently.** To help kids with LD and AD/HD understand and obey the rules, it's essential to reinforce them regularly. Keep rules simple and short, and post them in highly visible places.

- **Review last week's or last month's lesson.** Briefly review the Bible story from last week or the content of last week's children's sermon. Reviewing helps everyone remember and build on what they've learned. Reviewing also helps kids with LD and AD/HD to focus on the day's theme and lesson.

- **Use follow-up directions.** Follow verbal directions with a visual cue by holding up the book or writing down the page number, Scripture text, or hymn number on the board. Take the time to see that everyone is where they need to be. This simple check allows both visual and auditory learners to keep up with the group.

- **Use a variety of methods and media.** Keeping in mind that we all learn in different ways, use audiotapes or CDs, tangible objects, videos, pictures, and computer games to help kids engage the lesson or story. Use concrete examples, particularly with kids who have difficulty with abstract thought. Telling stories, or having kids write or tell stories, can also be an effective way to learn for children and youth with LD and AD/HD. Encourage the use of creative arts to engage kids in church school or worship. Drama, dance, movement, music, and/or video recording call on a wide variety of individual strengths in learning and worship and accommodate a variety of skills and abilities in affirming ways.

- **Use positive reinforcement.** On many days, kids with LD and AD/HD may not have much to celebrate or feel proud about. So participating in the congregation's worship and education ministry needs to be a positive experience for them and for their families. Teachers can help by pointing out accomplishments, activities, or projects kids have done well. Of course, it's important to praise honestly, not insincerely. Affirm kids whenever you can—it brings out the best in everyone. And pointing out what's good about your kids gives them—and their families—something to be proud of.

- **Develop a network of support.** Because low self-esteem is such an issue with children and youth with LD and AD/HD, developing a support system can help them participate in the congregation's education and worship ministries. Experts, including Newman and Webb-Mitchell, encourage congregations to identify and train adults who relate well to young people and are willing to serve as friends or mentors. Depending on the child's needs, the friend could accompany him or her to Sunday school class or worship, participate in special programs, or act as a sounding board about life and faith issues. Partnering with such an adult mentor can help young people with LD and AD/HD stay on task, behave appropriately, and participate in group activities. In addition, these mentors can help kids find appropriate, non-disruptive ways to share their insights with the rest of the class. Keep in mind that the support of adult mentors or friends need not be limited to the church setting; there may be opportunities to help out at home as well.

- **Celebrate achievements.** Congregational life includes a number of occasions for the community to celebrate. Children make the honor roll, graduate from high school, or receive a scholarship or award—all of which are mentioned in the church newsletter or bulletin. Acknowledging the achievements of members allows all to join together in the celebration.

Children and youth with LD and AD/HD and their families may have fewer such celebrations than other families—in part because the kinds of things these families celebrate are not often recognized by the wider community. Passing a class or a grade; having a day free of conflict; making progress in abstract thinking; or learning to read (or write or do mathematical computations) are generally taken for granted, and therefore thought to be unworthy of celebration. Other potential causes of celebration—the successful completion of a behavior contract at school; an effective and helpful change in medication; or making progress with a tutor to keep or regain grade-level status—are not celebrated because they are seen as private or even as a potential source of embarrassment to children and their families.

We encourage you to explore ways to become more inclusive in the events your congregation celebrates and acknowledges. This will vary from community to community. The key thing to remember is that achievements worthy of celebration vary widely according to the members of the congregation. Just as we weep with those who weep, we in the baptized community need to rejoice with those who rejoice (Rom. 12:15)—for whatever reason.

- **Share information with other children and youth.** Barbara Newman makes this key recommendation in her book *Helping Kids Include Kids with Disabilities*. Newman cites her own hearing loss as an example. While noting that there may be some discomfort in telling others about one's disability, she explains that the benefit of having people know she has a hearing impairment (so they don't mistake her lack of response to auditory cues as rudeness or disapproval) overrides her unease.

  All children need to be taught to be sensitive and inclusive. They need, as Newman puts it, "the right glasses" with which to see and understand why a classmate acts and reacts the way she or he does in the classroom. The understanding that comes with accurate information helps us all to respond with compassion rather than judgment. In order to share effectively while preserving family privacy, it's essential to seek permission from parents before any in-class conversation about a classmate's disabilities. Not all parents will want their child's disability to be shared with his or her class; in such cases, of course, teachers must respect that decision.

  Newman's book includes information and helpful suggestions for sharing information with children on a wide variety of disabilities, including LD and AD/HD. Such sharing typically takes place with the child present, so she can answer questions and speak for herself. As well, parents of kids with LD and of other children in the class need to be informed of any accommodations made in the class. Open discussion about differences and accommodation can diffuse many classroom tensions before they occur. Remember, though, that sharing information about a child's disabilities must be approached with great sensitivity, and only with full cooperation and permission from the child's family.

- **Finally, remember the good things.** Often we focus on the problems of children and youth with LD and AD/HD. We need remind ourselves to remember and to look for the gifts these children and youth bring to the church community. This focus will give us a renewed focus on the goal of our ministry—growth in Christ for all we serve.

Accommodations in the Setting

This section on accommodations has to do with the physical setting of your ministry program: the building, walls, floors, furniture, and lighting. It includes the technologies and educational tools and resources employed. Most important, in this section we address the attitudes and perspectives of your church community.

- **Develop a culture of acceptance.** As your congregation develops its ministry to and with children and youth with LD and AD/HD and their families, acceptance of difference must become the norm. Members of the congregation must come to identify with and invest in this acceptance.

  At first, many of the accommodations that you try may cause some discomfort and engender resistance. But over time, these efforts to become more hospitable will become noticeable. Members and church leaders will begin to experience some of the good changes resulting from these accommodations. This is the beginning of cultural transformation. The ultimate goal in your ministry is to create a culture of acceptance of difference that is welcoming of others and is observable to those inside and outside the church community. Cultural change is neither an easy nor a short-term process. It involves some difficult steps—steps that may cause real conflict and even at times a sense of loss for the way things used to be. For some members, the suggested accommodations will be risky and will require time to be accepted. Seeking God's guidance as a congregation is essential as you move forward in this ministry. You'll find helpful resources for further study in the Appendices of this book.

  Finally, remember that children and youth with LD and AD/HD and their families often approach congregational ministry with some wariness. Some of these families have had bad experiences in other settings. Many of them will judge the authenticity and depth of the welcome you offer. But offer it we must; for Jesus calls us to welcome these children and their families in his name.

- **Adjust seating.** This strategy will sound familiar to parents who have more than one child. To make a long car trip bearable and increase sibling harmony, mom and dad have kids change seats regularly. Children and youth with LD and AD/HD can often sit comfortably and (somewhat more) quietly beside certain people. However, sitting beside other people, often their friends, almost guarantees classroom disruption. That's because these kids "feed off" each others' learning challenges. So it's important to separate children with similar challenges during an activity.

Adjusted seating, sometimes referred to as *strategic seating,* means that teachers and worship leaders intentionally think through where kids will be best able to participate. That means planning where specific children and youth will sit in the classroom and sanctuary. Some students will need to sit next to the teacher or in a pew close to the worship leader. Others will need a trained adult friend to accompany them each Sunday in worship or in each class (see p. 39).

- **Create small spaces free of distractions.** Some children and youth with LD and AD/HD cannot function well in the large, open spaces of many church school classrooms and worship spaces. Their ability to focus is impaired to the point that they cannot participate effectively in the regular classroom or sanctuary with all the attendant noise, colors, sights, and sounds.

  These kids need a space where they (perhaps with their adult friend) can successfully participate in learning and/or worship. This may require creative thinking, as most church settings don't readily provide such a quiet space. Perhaps setting aside a corner of the room, or placing a table between the child and the rest of the group will work. Be open to using separate lessons and worship activities or allowing the child to work separately but within the teacher's sight. This kind of accommodation takes some extra thought and planning, both in providing an appropriate physical setting and in adapting activities to a child who is separated from the rest of the group. But it is well worth the extra effort to enable these children to participate in Sunday school and worship, and to find a sense of belonging in God's family.

- **Review use of wall space.** Take a look at the walls of the classroom. Are learning activities, banners, posters, and announcements from last week—or last month—still posted on the walls? Be aware that many children and youth with LD and AD/HD will find these distracting. Limit the use of walls, bulletin boards, and chalkboards to information or materials related to the lesson for the day.

- **Use pointers and tracking devices to help with reading.** Adult friends can assist with this accommodation. You'll need to provide a bookmark (those with Bible verses or affirming messages are readily available at Christian bookstores) or ruler for each child and make sure the adult friend knows how to assist him or her to use it to follow along with the text.

- **Turn off the lights when it's time to move.** Signal a transition to the class by turning off the lights. This gives everyone the same signal and enables children and youth with LD and AD/HD to work toward the transition. Younger children respond well to a clean-up song or familiar music played to indicate a transition.

- **Look into alternative lighting.** The hum of fluorescent lights can be distracting to some students. In addition, fluorescent lighting in schools has been linked to increased hyperactivity, stress, depression, fatigue, and irritability in students (Laurence D. Martel, "Light: An Element in the Ergonomics of Learning," www.intellearn.org). Look into the possibility of installing incandescent or the newer low-energy lights for use in classrooms and worship spaces.

- **Use available technologies.** Computers, PowerPoint presentations, DVDs and videos, CD players, and other technologies can be great tools for education and worship. Using a variety of media can help avoid boredom and assist students with learning challenges to engage the material.

- **Investigate the impact of music.** For some children and youth with LD and AD/HD, the sound of music playing quietly in the background is soothing and helps them focus; for others it is a big distraction. Pay attention to how students in your class respond to the use of music both as teaching tools and as background sound.

- **Monitor the noise level.** Be sensitive to the general level of noise in the classroom and in the sanctuary. Remember that children and youth with LD and AD/HD often have difficulty screening out distractions, including noise levels. Do what you can to reduce internal and external room noise and work with building staff or the building committee to find solutions.

- **Reduce staff changes.** This accommodation may come as an unwelcome shock to many Christian education committees who have adopted the trend of employing teacher teams who share responsibility of teaching a class and other models, such as the rotation model, that employ a variety of staff and class venues each week.

These popular approaches certainly have advantages. The team teaching model allows those who cannot commit to teaching every Sunday (or every week) to participate in the Sunday school ministry. Teaching teams set their own teaching schedule. Responsibility is shared and more people are able to serve. For many congregations, this approach has allowed them to continue Christian education ministries in ways not possible using more traditional models.

Similarly, the rotation model has animated Sunday school programs in many congregations with exciting options presented in different rooms. In some ways, the rotation model is like the older "learning centers" model. On any given Sunday, a class could rotate to a computer Bible study game, or building a Bible time village, or baking unleavened bread, or hearing a Bible story. The number of centers varies depending on the number of staff, space available, and the number of kids served.

As we seek to offer authentic hospitality to children and youth with LD and AD/HD and their families, we need to remind ourselves of these givens for many of them:

- Transitions are difficult.

- Focus is difficult.

- They are easily distracted.

- They take more time to adjust to a new person, room, or activity.

- Structure and routine are essential.

- Building relationships is difficult.

These considerations should guide your choice of options. These options include

- using the traditional model of having one or two teachers for each class, who are present for most if not all class sessions all year long.

- training adult friends to seek other options and activities when a class session is not working for his or her young friend.

- offering some classes with the traditional model and channeling children and youth with LD and AD/HD into these.

- developing a different approach to educational ministry by discerning what it is that forms people into disciples and engaging people in faith formation through their participation in the life and worship of the congregation. Some confirmation programs for small numbers of students use a similar approach and could be replicated to suit your needs.

All of these options take time and thought. Locate resource persons who work with children and youth with LD and AD/HD to assist you in discerning what options might work best, considering your staff, space, and the children and youth you seek to serve.

Keep your eye on the goal of your entire educational ministry and include approaches that specifically reach children and youth with various abilities to become active members of Christ's body, the church. Seek God's guidance and strength in the changes you are called on to make, so that you may truly welcome all those who come through your doors.

Accommodations Children and Youth with LD and AD/HD Can Make for Themselves

Children and youth with LD and AD/HD can learn to make accommodations for themselves as needed. These accommodations need to start small, particularly with younger children. As children learn to advocate for themselves, self-accommodation can become a real boost to kids' self-esteem and an effective tool for ministry.

In schools, teaching children and youth with LD and AD/HD skills in self-accommodation is a significant emphasis, particularly as students get to higher elementary, middle school, and high school levels. But in congregational ministry, we have much less time with children and youth than they spend in school. To the extent that these strategies being taught in school are helpful to kids and their families, we can reinforce them as much as possible.

We encourage the following techniques for teaching self-accommodation and self-advocacy to be used with the whole class or group of children or youth. This way, the child with LD or AD/HD is not singled out. In addition, these strategies can help all children approach their learning and faith development more thoughtfully. These suggestions are revised and expanded from Grad Flick's *How to Reach and Teach Teenagers with ADHD,* page 158.

- **Teach kids to repeat instructions.** Teaching kids to repeat instructions immediately results in two things: first, teachers break down instructions into smaller segments so each can be repeated; and second, kids will refrain from impulsively starting to work before they understand what the teacher said.

- **Teach kids to ask for help as needed.** As you model acceptance of differences with your kids, accepting requests for help needs to become a normal part of the class. Children and youth learn from other contexts that asking "dumb questions" results in laughter and scorn. So you may have some retraining to do. Help children and youth to understand that the assumptions on which other communities are based are not the same as those in the body of Christ. Stress that in this community, we welcome and encourage all requests for help.

- **Teach kids to take a "time-out" whenever they need to.** Many children and youth with LD and AD/HD experience frustration in their attempts to learn and to fit in with a group. Sometimes this frustration erupts into outbursts—yelling, crying, throwing things, and even aggressive behavior directed at property or people. So it's important for kids to learn early in life the warning signals that may result in an outburst. You'll need to point out the need for good anger management to everyone in the class. Describe examples of situations in which kids have permission to take a "time-out."

For many children and youth with LD and AD/HD, awareness of the warning signals takes a long time to develop. When a circumstance is too difficult, a child may run out of the classroom—a dangerous situation that must be avoided. In addition to making sure these children have an adult friend or mentor in the class, there should always be two adults in the classroom who can assist the class with the trauma of this behavior. Planning ahead about how to manage such a situation includes knowing where a child's parents can be located in the building. Keeping the child with special needs and all other children safe is paramount.

Designate a safe space in the classroom for time-outs, and make sure everyone knows they are to leave the child in the time-out space alone. Explain that the point of a time-out is time alone in a safe place to deal with feelings of frustration. (Although there may be times this can be done with a quiet adult friend in attendance.)

Ministering to children and youth with serious anger management issues calls for clear policies on what to do and who will be involved should a child or youth lose control of her anger during a class. Children and youth who are at risk of losing control (and their families) need to be informed of the policy and how it will work. Self-accommodation for anger management issues depends on the sharing of accurate and consistent information with children and their families. Remember that the behavior of all children improves when guidelines for conduct and the consequences for misbehavior are clearly communicated to children and their parents.

- **Teach kids to solve problems in creative and positive ways.** Teachers can model this by responding to a dilemma in a Scripture text or story by leading the group in a problem-solving exercise. Offer a problem-solving method based on posing critical questions. Encourage kids to ask questions like these: What is the problem? Is there more than one way to solve it? Which solution is best? How would I choose to solve the problem, using this solution?

This method of problem-solving engenders discussion and encourages systematic thinking, which slows everyone down and reduces impulsivity. Finally, this strategy encourages children and youth to approach faith and life critically and to work together to come to good answers.

- **Teach kids how to organize their work into manageable sections.** We've already discussed how important structure, routine, and ritual are to children and youth with LD and AD/HD. In addition, lengthy and detailed assignments can easily overwhelm these kids. Teachers can help by dividing projects and assignments such as learning the books of the Bible or the New Testament timeline into manageable pieces. Everyone will benefit from developing this key skill for organizing life as well as classroom learning.

- **Teach kids to discern their gifts and to share them in ministry with others.** As leaders and teachers discern the particular gifts of children and youth in your congregation, it's important to find ways for them to share these gifts. Consider how children and youth can participate: perhaps by singing in their age-group choirs, reading Scripture, or sharing artistic or musical skills. Offer opportunities to participate in video production and computer technologies; encourage those who want to develop a PowerPoint presentation or a DVD of music or poetry for education or worship. The more children and youth participate in leadership, the more your congregation will come to accept and celebrate the wide variety of their gifts.

Accommodations Families Can Reinforce at Home

Home reinforcement of the learning and growth that takes place at church is an invaluable tool in achieving ministry goals. Many families of children and youth with LD and AD/HD want to help their child grow in faith through participation in your church. The synergy of using similar accommodations at home and in church can be powerfully transformative for children, youth, and families—and for your whole congregation.

Parents who have been actively engaged in advocating for their children's education for some time will approach the conversation about working with your congregation differently than those whose children have just been diagnosed or who do not have a diagnosis. For parents who are new to the intricacies of working to get the best education for their child with LD or AD/HD, we recommend exploring these websites: www.ldonline.org and www.wrightslaw.com. The LD Online site offers articles on everything from basic information to cutting-edge research. The Wrightslaw site deals with special education law and provides articles helpful to parents and those working toward more inclusive education and worship ministries.

This section outlines some accommodations in which parents can take part in their children's spiritual growth and health.

- **Pray at home.** This may sounds simple. But participating in the prayer life of the community by praying at home is powerful in many ways.

  First, families who pray together are part of the "sweet communion" of saints on earth and saints above of which the hymn writers speak. Through the act of praying, families unite with other members of the community who are in prayer. Children can learn to comprehend this mystery and to participate joyfully.

  Then, as children see their parents praying and join them in prayer, they learn what it means to be a mature Christian. They learn that prayer is what we do as people of faith. This kind of modeling reinforces well the learning that goes on in worship and in the Christian education classroom.

Finally, intercessory prayer needs to be a key strategy in our ministry with children and youth with LD and AD/HD, and their families. We need to stand with these families and these children in prayer. And as parents lead their children in prayer, they need the assurance that the community prays with them and for them.

- **Use ritual.** Children enjoy keeping family traditions. Sacred ritual is part of the church's tradition, and it can energize spiritual life in the home. Incorporate ritual at meals, on Sundays, and at holidays. Ritual can help establish a rhythm of spiritual health and wholeness to family life. In addition, ritual can help a child with LD or AD/HD to slow down and reduce impulsivity and anxiety about transitions such as bed time. Many of these kids are capable of leading ritual at home as well as in worship.

  By repeating the ritual phrases used in worship, families can reinforce the learning of all of the liturgical phrases and hymns used by your congregation, thus enabling their children to participate more confidently in congregational worship.

- **Discuss worship and Christian education at home.** Reviewing the topics addressed in worship and education ministries at home helps reinforce the learning that takes place there. Even if parents have questions about teaching, preaching, or liturgy, discussion of these points, particularly with older children and youth, encourages the development of critical thinking skills. Encourage parents to make conversing about church part of the weekly ritual at home. It's a step toward a healthy spiritual life for all family members.

- **Review the goals of the church's learning plan with your child.** Parents have goals for their children's spiritual life and faith journey. Ideally, the Christian education director will yearly review the family's goals and the list of necessary accommodations for each child. These times of review offer an opportunity to set new learning goals and strategies with the family's input. From time to time, parents should also review the goals and evaluate the accommodations with their child, so that they can suggest changes as appropriate and recommit themselves to working toward the goals.

- **Affirm your child's growth.** Every child needs affirmation. Children and youth with LD and AD/HD are no different than their peers in this respect—except that perhaps they need affirmation more from their families because of the added stress learning challenges bring to their lives. Parents are their children's primary teachers, role models, and examples in life. Regularly affirming your child's growth will help him or her in working toward the goals you have agreed on. It also increases self-esteem, which motivates and enables kids to learn and grow. In turn, Christian education staff can affirm parents in their parenting role and encourage ways to affirm their child.

- **Participate with your child in worship and education ministries.** This final accommodation for parents is perhaps the most important. All children learn best through the example set by their parents. Parents who participate in worship and congregational life teach their children that spiritual life is a high priority. Parental participation in worship is often the key to their children's successful involvement. Having their parents involved helps make Sunday school and worship a safe space for children and youth.

Finally, parents are a key part of the support system that enables kids to participate in activities such as youth group meetings, church camp, overnight activities, and service opportunities. Parent participation may allow children with LD and AD/HD to risk trying new things. The nature of parental participation will change as the child's needs and abilities develop and the church leadership becomes accustomed to making specific accommodations.

Conclusion

Over the past forty years, research about children and youth with LD and AD/HD has resulted in the development of effective strategies and accommodations. This, the longest chapter in the book, shares the good news we've learned about strategies that really work. We believe that there are many, many good people in congregations who deeply desire to minister to and with these children and youth in their faith communities. And we're convinced of the transformative impact you can have on these children and youth as you create a welcoming and safe space for them to grow in faith.

APPENDICES

APPENDIX A

Case Stories: Issues that Arise in Congregational Ministry

These true case stories outline some of the issues children with learning disabilities and their families face. All names and some details have been changed. Each of the stories is followed by discussion questions. You may use them as a helpful way to raise awareness of learning disability issues with church school teachers, Christian education committees, worship leaders, worship committees, congregation members, or members of a church board or church staff.

Permission is granted to photocopy these stories and questions for use in congregations.

Peter and the Youth Group Retreat

Peter is in grade 7. He has always been fascinated by Bible stories and knows many of them by heart, having spent a lot of time during worship services reading the Bible. Because of his knowledge of the Bible, Peter has been affirmed in Sunday school and is liked by his teachers.

At Peter's church, the seventh graders begin the youth group year by going away for a fall camping retreat. During the first youth group meeting, all seventh graders receive an information sheet and a permission slip for parents to sign.

Because Peter has had some disastrous experiences while sleeping away from home, he decides to throw away the information about the camping trip. So his mom is surprised the next Sunday when a youth group leader asks her about Peter's participation. In the car after church, Peter tells his parents that he doesn't want to go. He explains that he is embarrassed to take the meds he needs in front of others, and he doesn't want to repeat his earlier negative experiences. Peter's parents affirm his right to make his own decision on this matter, and they agree with the way he has made his choice.

Later that day, the youth group director calls Peter on the phone. Caught unaware, and not wanting to seem unpleasant, Peter agrees to go on the trip. This precipitates a crisis: Peter really doesn't want to stay overnight. He and his parents try to find a solution that would involve having his dad go along just for the day part of the trip. But as the campsite is located three hours away, they conclude that this is not a realistic option. Peter's dad then decides to resolve the situation by calling the director to inform him that Peter isn't going to go.

On the phone, the director tries to convince Peter's dad that this camping trip is crucial for forming community and relationships within the group. He encourages Peter's dad not to be too protective and assures him that Peter would undoubtedly have a wonderful time. In fact, he tells Peter's dad that it's time for him to "let go" so that Peter can "grow up." Trying hard to control his temper, and not wanting to share personal information that he feels is none of the youth director's business, Peter's dad cuts the phone call short by simply saying that Peter won't be going and hanging up.

For Discussion

1. Why did Peter, the youth director, and Peter's dad react the way they did? Discuss possible motivating factors.

2. What kinds of information would each person need to react in ways that might have led to a more positive outcome?

3. What issues does this story raise that need to be addressed by those planning congregational youth ministry?

4. In small groups discuss the following options for resolution of the issues raised in the story:

    (a) If Peter were to go on the trip, what would need to take place? What information would need to be shared? With whom would the information need to be shared, and when? What accommodations would be required for Peter to participate successfully?

    (b) If Peter does not go on the trip, what needs to happen so that his participation in the group does not suffer? What accommodations might allow Peter to participate in ways that engender mental, physical, and spiritual health and wholeness?

(c) What other options are possible for the trip itself that would make participation for children with LD and AD/HD more plausible and healthy? Who would need to be consulted? How much time would be needed for planning new forms of youth ministry that were inclusive of all who might want to participate?

Christina's Confirmation

Twelve-year-old Christina is in fifth grade. She has taken part in religious education since she was small. Although her learning disabilities have made consistent participation in church school difficult, she enjoys participating to the degree she can do so. Over the years Christina has experienced her church as a safe place where she feels a sense of community.

Christina's learning disabilities make it particularly hard for her to memorize text, which is a particular emphasis of the curriculum her church school uses. Christina also has difficulty with attention over an extended period of time, so she attends part of the worship service and then goes with an adult, either one of her parents or another member of the congregation, to another part of the building. There she reads, sings, prays, and draws or paints until worship is over.

The other kids who are Christina's age are in a special class this year with the pastor. They are preparing for the time when they will publicly profess their faith—called "confirmation" in her church. Christina's church has a special ritual for young people who are professing their faith, a ritual that involves memorizing and reciting text and sitting through an entire service until communion is celebrated at the end of the service.

Christina's mother approaches the pastor to discuss options for Christina's participation in confirmation. His response is to outline the entire confirmation ritual and give her a copy of the text to be memorized. The pastor encourages her to work with Christina at home as the other parents are doing with their children. When she expresses some doubt about Christina's ability to participate in a whole worship service, much less to stand in front of the entire congregation and recite memorized text with other children, the pastor encourages her to have more faith in her daughter. "I've seen a lot of kids in my day, Joan," he says. "No matter how nervous they are, they all come together in the end. Besides, she'll be up there with a whole group of her friends. Even if she's nervous, her friends' presence will make it better for her."

For Discussion

1. Discuss possible motivating factors for the pastor and Christina's mom in their discussion above.

2. What information needed to be shared so that the pastor and Christina's mom could discuss the situation constructively and come to some alternative solutions?

3. What is "fair" to expect of Christina in relationship to what the other children are doing?

4. Identify what issues are raised for congregational education and worship ministries in this case.

5. In small groups, discuss the following options for resolution of the issues raised:

> (a) If Christina were to participate in the service and be confirmed, what planning would be necessary? What issues would be raised for Christina, her family, the other children, and the congregation by Christina's participation? How much time would be needed to make a plan that would work for all involved? What kinds of people would be needed to help make the plan work? What accommodations would be necessary?

> (b) If Christina were not to participate in the service, what alternative plan could be devised so that she could be confirmed? Who would need to be involved in the planning for this alternative? What issues would be raised by Christina not taking part with her age group in the ritual?

> (c) How could congregations facilitate the participation of children and youth with LD and AD/HD in rituals like confirmation in ways that engender spiritual growth for both the children and the whole congregation? What steps would need to take place with the congregation, its staff, its leadership, and the congregation as a whole?

The Smiths Join Faith Church

Each summer, Faith Church sponsors a very well-attended program for elementary school-age children. Volunteers lead kids in Bible lessons, singing, arts and crafts, and daily field trips to the pool, the park, and the zoo.

Many people in the community take advantage of this summer program; in fact, a number of members were introduced to the congregation through this ministry. This past summer, Perry, Marcus, and Sarah Smith came with their dad to register for the program. Perry and Marcus had completed second and third grades, respectively; Sarah had finished kindergarten. The boys joined the grade 2-3 class; Sarah the kindergarten-grade 1 class.

Before long, staff began making comments about Perry and Marcus. Sometimes the boys would slip out of the classroom and run around the church building or grounds. Other times they would be silly in class, sometimes becoming nearly hysterical. Frequently one or the other would obsess about an object another child or a staff member was using and be willing to do just about anything to get it—including grabbing, manipulative behavior, and stealing. The brothers refused to read in class, either silently or aloud, and they didn't seem to be learning anything. When their dad picked the kids up at the end of each day (always late), the staff heaved a collective sigh of relief.

The day Perry grabbed a pair of scissors and he and Marcus started running around with them, the Christian education director felt she could no longer put off talking to Mr. Smith. When he arrived that afternoon, she asked to speak with him.

In the ensuing discussion, Mr. Smith apologized for the boys' behavior. He said that the kids' school had suggested testing, medication, and therapy. He had recently moved and changed jobs, and the kids' mother had moved out six months before. He was going through a divorce, had no insurance, and was working to keep things together. From his perspective, the children were simply reacting to the upheaval in their home, and he didn't believe that the boys needed to be medicated. In the director's presence, he threatened them with consequences if they didn't "shape up."

The boys' behavior moderated slightly for much of the rest of the summer, with occasional outbursts. But on the whole the staff believed that perhaps things were calming down for this family.

In the fall, the Smiths began attending worship regularly. Their attendance brought some of the summer program issues into worship. People began to suggest to the pastor that he should talk to Mr. Smith about "appropriate worship behavior." Conversations at church and in the home employed the same script and information that was shared during the summer. The boys' behavior in worship and Sunday school didn't improve, but Mr. Smith expressed to many members of the congregation how welcome he felt at the church. In October, Mr. Smith attended the new members' class, and in November he and the children joined the church. All three children were baptized. Meanwhile, complaints about Perry and Marcus to the pastoral staff continued to increase in severity and tone. The pastor and education director were at a loss when the Christian education committee voiced a question shared by many: "What are we going to do about the Smith boys? Now that we're stuck with them, how can we handle them?"

For Discussion

1. Identify the issues raised by this case. What are the issues raised for education ministry, worship ministry, and for the congregation as a whole?

2. Having studied LD and AD/HD, what is your best guess about what is going on with the Smith boys? What issues in the case either help relieve or exacerbate the problem(s)?

3. What advice would you give to the following people:

    (a) the Christian education director?

    (b) the pastor?

    (c) volunteers working with the summer program?

    (d) worship leaders?

4. What information needs to be shared so that the congregation can effectively and helpfully welcome the Smith family? Who needs to be involved in the sharing? Who needs to receive the information? What should be done with the information, once received?

5. What accommodations are called for by this case:

> (a) in education ministry?
>
> (b) in worship ministry?
>
> (c) in other ministries?

6. Where should the congregation go from here?

Annotated List of Scripture Texts for Preaching and Teaching Inclusion

As you will see from this representative sampling, it is not hard to find Scripture texts that provide bases for inclusive ministries. These texts could also be helpful as devotional Scriptures for personal reading, for educational ministry leaders, and for parent support groups. For more thorough treatment, a number of the texts included in the bibliography can assist the teacher, preacher, or worship leader.

Old Testament

- Genesis 1:27
  Since God created all persons in his image, people with disabilities should be included and integrated in the faith community.

- Genesis 18:1-8
  This passage points to the biblical mandate of hospitality, a virtue the faith community has often lacked in our approach to persons and families dealing with disability.

- **Proverbs 18:10**
  This proverb offers a vision of the strength and refuge afforded to the righteous, who "run" to the "strong tower" made by the name of the Lord for them. Can we build a place of safety and refuge in the Christian community for people with disabilities?

- **Isaiah 55:10-11**
  An assurance is given here to build the foundation for religious education for those with learning disabilities, as God's Word will "not return empty" to God, but will "accomplish that which [God] purposes" and "succeed in the thing" for which God sent it.

- **Isaiah 56:1-8**
  This prophecy deals with the mandated inclusion of the "stranger," the "foreigner," and the "eunuch." The passage preaches inclusivity that extends to those formerly cut off and cast out. The hospitality of those who worship this inclusive God must engage those who are cut off and cast out in our age, including people with disabilities.

- **Jeremiah 9:23-24**
  This prophetic word affirms that the key issue is not earthly understandings of wisdom, might, or wealth, but rather knowledge of the Lord, the One who "acts with steadfast love, justice and righteousness," for in these things the Lord delights. The ability of people with special needs to know God and to be a delight to the Lord in giving and receiving love, justice, and righteousness, affirms their place in the community.

- **Jeremiah 31:31-34**
  The knowledge of the Lord will not be limited to those who are "great"—which can mean strong, wise, or able—but extends also to those who are "the least of them." This suggests that ability is not a criterion that determines inclusion in the community.

New Testament

- **Matthew 7:12**
  Commonly known as the Golden Rule, this verse provides a foundation for inclusion and compassion for all.

- **Matthew 11:2-6**
  The coming of Jesus means healing and inclusion in the community for those who were formerly cut off.

- Matthew 25:31-46
  When we offer to "the least of these" what they require for wholeness and life, we offer the same gifts to Jesus.

- Luke 18:16-17
  Letting the children come to Jesus is a mandate that does not exclude those who have trouble getting to the place where believers gather.

- John 8:12
  All who follow Jesus have his light and do not live in darkness.

- Acts 10:34
  This passage is the climax of a story that takes up this entire chapter, in which Peter learns about the all-encompassing grace and love of God, which is extended even to the Gentiles. This same love and grace is extended to all who believe.

- Romans 2:11
  Another reference to God's inclusive grace, like Acts 10; could be used in combination with other similar texts.

- Romans 5:12-21
  Provides a foundation for a preaching or teaching series about the meaning of personhood, of being in Christ, which for many includes the experience of disability. Justification and life are available to all, through the grace of God in the free gift of Jesus Christ (see v. 18).

- Romans 8:38-39
  Nothing will be able to separate us from God's love; surely disabling conditions are on that list of "anything else in all creation."

- Romans 12:1-2
  The understanding of our bodies as "living sacrifices" that are to be "transformed by the renewing of [our] minds" has much to say to persons with disabilities, their families, and those with whom they share Christian community. Renewal of our minds does not depend on physical or mental ability but on the closeness with which we follow Christ.

- 1 Corinthians 1:26-31
  We who follow Jesus are called to be proud, not of our abilities, but of our Lord—so that if we boast we boast in Jesus. Indeed, this passage lifts up those who may be "low and despised" in the world as specifically chosen and used by God.

- **1 Corinthians 2:6-16**
  God does not depend on our wisdom and our strength to make things happen; in fact, God chooses what is weak and foolish to show God's strength and wisdom. Therefore, being a child of God does not depend on what we can do or how we can learn.

- **1 Corinthians 12**
  The scriptural list of the parts of the body that all must work together so that God's work can be done includes those with every kind of ability and challenge.

- **1 Corinthians 13**
  Our ability to give and receive Christ's love is the highest form of service in God's kingdom.

- **Galatians 5:22-23**
  All believers produce the fruit of the Spirit described here. Because we are known by our fruit, people at all ability and challenge levels can show that they "belong to Christ Jesus."

- **Colossians 2:6-7**
  Living our life in Christ Jesus depends on being rooted and built up in Christ in the Christian community.

APPENDIX C

Ideas for Celebrating Access and Inclusion in Your Congregation

1. Create a PowerPoint presentation with pictures of symbols of access and inclusion in and around your church. These might include the following:

   - sign from the handicapped parking place

   - elevator, entrance ramp, chair lift, and/or ramps that allow people to go from one area of the building to another

   - certificate that states that your building is barrier-free

   - large-print bulletins and newsletters, Bibles, hymnals

   - participation in worship, education, and other congregational ministries of persons with disabilities

   - listening devices for the hearing impaired

   - section of your sanctuary set aside for those in wheelchairs

   - changes made in your worship space, classrooms, offices, restrooms, kitchen, fellowship space to accommodate wheelchairs

- signs that indicate fragrance-free worship service and/or classes
- tape ministry that shares worship with those who can't be physically present
- radio ministry
- taking communion to shut-ins and those not able to attend worship
- person who interprets the worship service or education ministry in American Sign Language
- adult friends who serve children and youth with LD and AD/HD
- celebrating rituals in classrooms and worship
- participation and leadership of those with disabilities
- creative arts in worship and education ministries
- computer learning center
- respite care program for parents and caregivers of persons with disabilities
- workshops with area LD and AD/HD resource persons, such as special education staff, researchers from the local university, or representatives from local chapters of learning disability organizations

2. Use music, art, drama, dance, and/or film in a celebration worship service, working to engage a variety of learning and worship styles.

3. Ask children and youth (with peers or adult friends) to participate in leading worship in ways that affirm their gifts. This might include anything from reading Scripture, praying, making an artistic offering, or writing a poem or psalm together.

4. Invite teachers and worship leaders who have been trained and have experienced the ways in which the congregation's welcome is growing wider to share their testimony.

5. Use the list of Scripture texts in Appendix B for inspiration to create new songs, prayers, psalms, or meditations.

6. Check the index of your hymnal to look for hymns based on the texts in Appendix B and use them in worship (such as "Your Hand, O Lord, in Days of Old," *Psalter Hymnal* 363; "Healer of Our Every Ill," *Sing! A New Creation* 205).

7. Use "An Interfaith Litany for Wholeness" in the service. Download it from the website of the National Organization on Disability (www.nod.org). Click on "Religious Participation," then click on the link for the litany. Also available in a printer-friendly version.

8. Use the video *Misunderstood Minds* (produced by WGBH Boston, available from www.pbs.org) as the basis for an adult and/or youth class that introduces your new ministry initiatives to welcome children and youth with learning disabilities and their families. In each session, watch a portion of the video together then discuss the issues raised for your ministry.

9. To prepare for the celebration, perform an audit of barriers in your congregation and church facility from the National Organization on Disability (same site as above; click on "Perform an Audit of Barriers"). The audit is also available in the NOD's book *That All May Worship: An Interfaith Welcome for People with Disabilities,* revised and expanded in 2005. Ordering information is available on the website.

Once you have done the audit, include a report of the findings in the celebration. This could take the form of a Minute for Access, a bulletin insert, or an information table set up before or after the service. This information could also be presented and discussed in the adult and/or youth class that uses the video *Misunderstood Minds* (see 8, above) as its foundational curriculum.

APPENDIX D

Helpful Websites

The following list includes many websites that have been used to research this volume. These sites were operational at the time of publication.

- www.access-board.gov/adaag/html/adaag.htm
  Guidelines about how to comply with the Americans with Disabilities Act (ADA) Accessibility Guidelines for Buildings and Facilities. With plenty of technical information available, this is the "go-to" site when your congregation is seriously ready to tackle building access issues.

- www.acdl.com
  Arizona Center for Disability Law; offers a lot of information on disability law, particularly in Arizona but also nationally. Includes workshops for Arizona residents and links for persons interested in advocacy or struggling to get services for themselves or others.

- www.adawatch.org
  National Coalition for Disability Rights; an advocacy and watchdog site urging action and awareness of disability legal issues.

- www.additudemag.com
  Online journal about attention deficit disorders in children, youth, and adults; offers a free e-newsletter, or you can subscribe to the magazine. Lots of helpful links.

- www.beaconcollege.edu
  Site of a liberal arts college in Florida that serves students with learning disabilities. Associate and bachelor's degrees available.

- http://ca.dir.yahoo.com/Society_and_Culture/Disabilities/
  Types_of_Disabilities/Learning_Disabilities
  A clearinghouse for information on learning disabilities in Canada. The site includes websites for associations, informational sites, institutions, and government agencies. Click on "Canada Listings Only" to be directed to Canadian resources and organizations.

- www.campkodiak.com
  Site of Camp Kodiak, a summer camp near Mississauga, Ontario, for sixteen- to eighteen-year-old youth with LD and AD/HD. Focus is on strengthening social skills.

- http://Canadian.cec.sped.org/
  Site of the Canadian Council for Exceptional Children, whose purpose is to advance the education of all exceptional children and youth— those with disabilities and those who are gifted. Site originates in the United States.

- www.cec.sped.org
  Council for Exceptional Children; sponsors research, publications, and conferences for educators and researchers in the field. Includes links to many of different kinds of articles.

- http://www.cfc-efc.ca
  Site of Child and Family Canada; a virtual consortium of 53 credible nonprofit organizations with expertise in issues relating to children and families. Includes a library of over 1,300 bilingual documents organized by theme and title.

- www.chadd.org
  Children and Adults with Attention Deficit/Hyperactivity Disorder.
  This organization has a long history, and the site has many helpful
  links. The organization is involved in advocacy and research and offers
  accurate and regularly updated information on AD/HD.

- www.clcnetwork.org
  The Christian Learning Center specializes in supporting children and
  adults with special needs both in Christian school and church settings.
  They offer partnerships with schools and churches in setting up programs
  and support to help meet individuals' needs while using their gifts.

- www.dldcec.org
  Council on Exceptional Children's Division for Learning Disabilities.
  A research-centered site for educators; offers good ideas and research
  about new techniques as well as news of legal issues in the field and
  conference announcements.

- www.drhallowell.com
  Site of Dr. Edward Hallowell, author of *Driven to Distraction*. Hallowell
  works particularly with AD/HD in children and adults. Helpful
  newsletter and conferences. Hallowell works in the Boston area and has
  just opened another center in California.

- www.ed.gov
  U.S. Department of Education site offers information on federal
  statutes and programs for persons with disabilities.

- www.ed.gov/about/offices/list/ies/ncser/index.html
  Newly created National Center for Special Education Research of the
  U.S. Department of Education. The Center was founded as part of the
  reauthorization of the Individuals with Disabilities Education Act of
  2004; the director was named in May 2005.

- www.eparent.com
  Online journal Exceptional Parent.com is a resource for parents of children with disabilities. Free registration allows access to information on
  research into a wide variety of disabilities including LD and AD/HD.

- http://www.eric.ed.gov
  Educational Resources Information Center, a project of the Institute for Education Services of the U.S. Department of Education. Offers a compendium of over one million resources (including articles, books, and web-based resources) published from 1966 to the present. Database includes many articles available previously on fee-based services only. The service, known in the field as the ERIC Clearinghouse, is free. Although you can register to design a site entrance that is tailored to your specific needs and interests, registration is not required to search the database nor to download articles.

- www.faithandlight.org
  English-language website of Faith and Light International, also known as Foi et Lumiere International, Jean Vanier, cofounder. The organization, related to the L'Arche Communities, offers support to persons with developmental disabilities in over 1,400 Christian communities, most of which are Roman Catholic. Access to Christian community and sacramental life are key emphases. Includes links to other sites and some good resource publications. Eastern U.S. chapters were featured in a 2005 *Washington Post* article available at www.washingtonpost.com/ac2/A22073-2005Apr2.html.

- www.friendship.org
  Friendship Ministries is an interdenominational, international ministry for people with cognitive impairments. Through consultation and with the help of resources that encourage spiritual development and relationships, Friendship Ministries helps churches to include people with congitive impairments in fellowship and service as members of the body of Christ.

- www.heath.gwu.edu
  George Washington University Heath Resource Center, a national clearinghouse on post-secondary education for individuals with disabilities. Includes information on how to find, apply for, and finance college education for disabled persons and on pre-college preparatory programs; many links to helpful organizations. The site is partially funded by the U.S. government.

- www.kidsource.com
  Online resource that has compiled articles on a wide variety of parenting subjects, including LD and AD/HD. Click on Education on the homepage, and then navigate your way to the subjects and articles that interest you.

- www.landmarkcollege.edu
  Landmark College in Vermont serves students with learning disabilities. Offers associate degrees.

- www.ldanatl.org
  Learning Disabilities Association of America, another good overview site with many helpful links.

- www.ldao.ca
  Learning Disabilities Association of Ontario. Includes helpful information and links, many in French.

- www.ldonline.org
  LD Online, a great site to introduce yourself to the topic. Links to articles on many topics and subheadings within the field. The papers of the National Joint Committee on Learning Disabilities (NJCLD) are published exclusively on LDOnline. This interdisciplinary committee of educators and mental health professionals, formed in 1975, has been offering cutting-edge research and conferences for the last thirty years.

- www.ldonline.org/finding_help/Canada.html
  This site (which can also be found as a link on the site above) includes organizations and agencies serving Canadian children, youth, and families, as well as Canada-specific resources.

- www.ldresources.com
  Operated by the University of Connecticut, this site offers opportunity for online dialogue between researchers and educators. Others are welcome to participate.

- www.luthsped.org
  Lutheran Special Education Ministries; works particularly with Lutheran and other Christian schools to develop appropriate educational plans for children with a variety of learning challenges. Offers consultants who work with congregations on developing different approaches for Sunday school or Vacation Bible School. Their national office and Resource Center is in Detroit.

- www.masscouncilofchurches.org/docs/accessibility.htm
  Massachusetts Council of Churches; site developed by the Council's Accessible Church committee. Good information on making your facility and ministry truly accessible to all.

- www.nafim.org
  The National Apostolate for Inclusion Ministry, a Roman Catholic organization serving the church and persons with cognitive impairments, developmental disability, and autism. Offers conferences and a wide variety of resources, including a list of resource persons who can staff events.

- www.ncld.org
  National Center for Learning Disabilities, a good overview site.

- www.neads.ca
  NEADS advocates for increased accessibility at all levels so that students with disabilities may gain equal access to college or university education. Canadian site.

- www.nidcd.nih.gov
  The National Institute on Deafness and other Communication Disorders offers information on auditory issues.

- www.nod.org
  National Organization on Disability; check out the "Religion and Disability Program" in which the National Council of Churches partners with NOD.

- www.pcusa.org/phewa/pdc.htm
  Presbyterians for Disabilities Concerns. Helpful links for use in developing Access Sunday celebrations; a list of consultants; and news of national conferences every two years.

- www.pwd-online.ca/pwdhome.jsp?lang_en
  Persons with Disabilities Online Canada, an organization that provides services to persons with disabilities and their families in Canada. Bilingual site.

- www.rrf.org/forapplicants/accessiblefaith.html
  Retirement Research Foundation's Accessible Faith Grant Program. Offers grants to assist in making Chicago area houses of worship accessible to elderly persons and to persons with disabilities.

- www.schoolnet.ca/sne/
  The Special Needs Education Network provides Internet services specific to parents, teachers, schools, and other professionals, individuals, groups, and organizations involved in the education of students with special needs. The Special Needs Education Network is a service provided under the auspices of the SchoolNet project, a cooperative initiative of Canada's provincial, territorial, and federal governments, in consultation with educators, universities, colleges, and industry.

- www.schwablearning.org
  Schwab Foundation for Learning, an arm of the Charles and Helen Schwab Foundation. The website is available in English or Spanish; includes links to resources, experts, research on LD and AD/HD.

- www.sdc.gc.ca/en/gateways/nav/top_nav/program/odi.shtml
  Office of Disability Issues, an agency of the Canadian government that works to "promote the full participation of Canadians with disabilities in learning, work and community life." Overview information of Canadian government initiatives and funding; helpful links. Bilingual.

- http://snow.utoronto.ca
  Website of SNOW, Special Needs Opportunities Windows, an excellent Canadian resource on special education needs and technologies. Extensive online resource lists.

- www.sparktop.org/intro.html
  A fun site for eight- to twelve-year-olds with learning disabilities. Offers games, music, cartoons, places for kids to express themselves through art and dialogue, and accurate information. Kids can win prizes, learn about their disabilities, and connect with other kids with learning disabilities. Kids offering kids no-nonsense advice!

- www.utoronto.ca/atrc
  Site of the Adaptive Technology Resource Center at the University of Toronto, which actively promotes inclusionary design in information networks. The centre works closely with education, government, industry, and organizational partners to increase accessibility and awareness of access issues. ATRC also provides information, demonstrations, and training in the use of access technology to educators, students, the media, and the general public.

- www.wrightslaw.com
  A great resource with information on federal special education law in the U.S. Many links and articles, including links to state associations that deal with special education law in their states, and links to state governmental agencies responsible for administration of special education services and enforcement of state education law.

Note: for Canadian information, check out www.ldac-taac.ca/LDandtheLaw/ch01_Law-e.asp. This is a link on the Learning Disabilities Association of Canada site called "Learning Disabilities and the Law: A Canadian Resource." Good overview of legal issues and lots of helpful links to legal statues and more.

BIBLIOGRAPHY

Books

Berryman, Jerome W. *Godly Play: An Imaginative Approach to Religious Education.* Minneapolis: Augsburg, 1991. One of the works built on the pioneering work of Maria Montessori and Sofia Cavalletti; a Montessori approach to Christian education that has been shown to be effective with some children with disabilities.

Black, Kathy. *A Healing Homiletic: Preaching and Disability.* Nashville: Abingdon Press, 1996. A good resource for preachers and teachers.

Bolduc, Kathleen Deyer. *A Place Called Acceptance: Ministry with Families of Children with Disabilities.* PCUSA: Louisville, KY, 2001. A short introduction to ways the Christian community can offer authentic welcome to persons with disabilities; includes many practical tips.

Cavalletti, Sofia. *The Religious Potential of the Child: Experiencing Scripture and Liturgy with Young Children.* Chicago: Liturgy Training Publications, 1992. Cavalletti built on the foundation of Maria Montessori to develop her Christian education program "The Catechesis of the Good Shepherd," still in place in many Catholic parishes worldwide.

Eiesland, Nancy L. *The Disabled God: Toward a Liberatory Theology of Disability.* Nashville: Abingdon Press, 1994.

Eiesland, Nancy L. and Don Saliers, eds. *Human Disability and the Service of God: Reassessing Human Practice.* Nashville: Abingdon Press, 1998. Eiesland, a person with disabilities, has pioneered in the theology of disabilities. She challenges the Christian community to make our welcome more authentic by putting money and energy where our rhetoric—and the gospel—would lead us. Written primary for the professional theologian.

Fishburn, Janet F. *Parenting is for Everyone: Living out Our Baptismal Covenant.* Louisville, KY: Presbyterian Mariners, 1996. Fishburn encourages every member of the community to live into the vows we make to children and families at baptism. A very practical book with lesson plans and learning activities.

Flick, Grad L. *How to Reach and Teach Teenagers with ADHD.* West Nyack, NY: The Center for Applied Research in Education, 2000. Flick is a major writer in the area of education for children and youth with ADHD. This large volume is filled with very practical ideas aimed at the public school classroom.

Fritzon, Anne and Samuel Kabue. *Interpreting Disability: Persons with Disabilities and the Church.* Geneva: WCC Publications, 2004. This short book offers both Western and African Christian perspectives on the reality of disability and the approach of the church.

Govig, Stewart D. *Strong at the Broken Places: Persons with Disabilities and the Church.* Louisville, KY: Westminster John Knox Press, 1989.

Hallowell, Edward. *A Walk in the Rain with a Brain.* New York: HarperCollins, 2004. A wonderfully colorful and imaginative book for children, explaining in a funny way that "no brain is best" and everyone's "smart" at something. A great resource to use with classes of children or in worship.

Halpin, Marlene. *Puddles of Knowing: Engaging Children in Our Prayer Heritage.* Dubuque, IA: Wm. C. Brown Company, 1984. Halpin is a nun who leads prayer ministry in Roman Catholic grade schools. This small book has many innovative ideas that can be used to slow down and focus impulsive learners.

Harris, Maria. *Fashion Me a People: Curriculum in the Church.* Louisville, KY: Westminster John Knox Press, 1989. This book is a classic in the field of ecclesiology as well as education. Harris explores what it is that we do as the body of Christ, what makes of us the body and what practices constitute us in community. A powerful work aimed primarily at theologically trained readers.

Levine, Mel. *A Mind at a Time.* New York: Simon and Schuster, 2002. Levine, a medical doctor with a practice aimed at diagnostic testing of children with learning challenges, maintains that each mind is different and every single child learns differently than any other. A thought-provoking book with good ideas that may have application in congregations. Levine is also featured on the PBS video/DVD, *Misunderstood Minds* (see p. 80).

Merrick, Lewis H., ed. *And Show Steadfast Love: A Theological Look at Grace, Hospitality, Disabilities and the Church.* Louisville, KY: PC(USA), 1993. A group of articles by theologians and biblical scholars on approaching the reality of disability theologically.

Montessori, Maria. *The Discovery of the Child.* New York: Ballantine Books, 1967. The work in which Montessori outlined her sense of children's potential. A classic.

Newman, Barbara J. *Helping Kids Include Kids with Disabilities.* Grand Rapids, Mich.: Faith Alive Christian Resources, 2001. Newman has packed a lot into a small book. A very practical guide to introducing the subject of disabilities with children in Christian schools and congregations. Lots of sample forms, information sheets, letters to parents, and much more.

Stewart, Sonja M. and Jerome W. Berryman. *Young Children and Worship.* Louisville: Westminster John Knox Press, 1989.

Stewart, Sonja M. *Following Jesus: More about Young Children and Worship.* Louisville: Geneva Press, 2000. These two books have been used by thousands of congregations, starting a global movement of worship and education for children.

Taylor, John F. *Helping Your Hyperactive/ADD Child.* Revised 3rd Edition. New York: Three Rivers Press, 2001. This book, written for parents, is full of helpful information and ideas. Many of these ideas can be of assistance in congregations as well as in the home and at school.

Thornburgh, Ginny, ed. *That All May Worship: An Interfaith Welcome to People with Disabilities.* Washington, DC: National Organization on Disability, 2005.

_____. *Loving Justice: The ADA and the Religious Community.*

_____. *From Barriers to Bridges: A Community Action Guide for Congregations and People with Disabilities.* These three guides, published by and available from the National Organization on Disability, help congregations find practical ways to open their doors to persons with disabilities.

Webb-Mitchell, Brett. *God Plays Piano Too: The Spiritual Lives of Disabled Children.* New York: Crossroad, 1993.

_____. *Unexpected Guests at God's Banquet: Welcoming People with Disabilites into the Church.* New York: Crossroad, 1994.

_____. *Dancing with Disabilities: Opening the Church to All God's Children.* Cleveland: United Church Press, 1996

_____. *Christly Gestures: Learning to be Members of the Body of Christ.* Grand Rapids, Mich.: Eerdmans, 2003. Webb-Mitchell has become a major figure in the field of theology of disability. His highly readable works have transformed the way that many congregations approach disabled children, youth and adults. Particularly notable is his idea that we should move away from "development" as our main approach in education and worship ministries and move toward "pilgrimage" instead.

Weiss Block, Jennie. *Copious Hosting: A Theology of Access for People with Disabilities.* New York: Continuum, 2002. Weiss Block is a community activist, working to increase access to people with disabilities. This very readable text, written by someone outside the theological academy, can be a helpful resource for study groups in congregations.

Journals

A number of good journals address disability issues. Some of these are listed below. Others can be found on an Internet or public library or university search.

- *Additude.mag,* for children, youth and adults with ADD and ADHD.

- *Exceptional Children,* published by the Council for Exceptional Children.

- *Learning Disabilities,* published by the Learning Disability Association of America.

- *Learning Disabilities: A Contemporary Journal,* published by Learning Disabilities Worldwide.

- *Learning Disability Quarterly,* published by the Council for Exceptional Children.

- *Teaching Exceptional Children,* published by the Council for Exceptional Children.

Journal Articles

Arnold, Nicki G. "Learned Helplessness and Attribution for Success and Failure in LD Students," reprinted from *Their World* by LDOnline, www.ldonine.org/ld_indepth/self_esteem/helplessness.html.

Baum, Susan. "Gifted but Learning Disabled: A Puzzling Paradox," reprinted from ERIC Digest by KidSource, www.kidsource.com/kidsource/content/Gifted_learning_disabled.html.

Clark, Margaret D. "Teacher Response to Learning Disability: A Test of Attributional Principles," reprinted from *Journal of Learning Disabilities* by LDOnline, www.ldonline.org/ld_indepth/self_esteem/teacherresponse.html.

Conover, Lynda. "Gifted and Learning Disabled? It Is Possible!," reprinted from Virginia Association for the Education of the Gifted by LDOnline, www.ldonline.org/ld_indepth/gt_ld/conover.html.

Cordoni, Barbara. "A Learning Disability Is Only One Part of a Child," from Newsbriefs, Learning Disabilities Association of America, reprinted by LDOnline, http://www.ldonline.org/ld_indepth/parenting/one_part.html.

Diller, Lawrence H. "The Run on Ritalin: Attention Deficit Disorder and Stimulant Treatment in the 1990s," Hastings Center Report, firstsearch.oclc.org/images/SWPL/wsppdfl/HTML/03045/AHXOR/GS9.HTM.

Garber, Benjamin D. "ADHD or Not ADHD: Custody and Visitation Considerations," healthyparent.com/adhd-divorce.html.

Grossman, Judy. "Family Matters: The Impact of Learning Disabilities," Smart Kids with Learning Disabilities, Inc., reprinted by LDOnline, http://www.ldonline.org/ld_indepth/family/familymatters.html.

Federal Bureau of Investigation U.S. Government, "ADHD and Implications for the Criminal Justice System,, www.mental-health-matters.com/articles/print.php?artID=682.

Ferguson, Philip M. "A Place in the Family: A Historical Interpretation of Research on Parental Reactions to Having a Child with Disability," from *The Journal of Special Education,* reprinted by LDOnline, /www.ldonline.org/ld_indepth/parenting/parental_reactions.html.

Hoffman, Heinrich, "The Story of Fidgety Philip," www.fln.vcu.edu/struwwel/philipp_e.html.

Neihart, Maureen. "Gifted Children with Attention Deficit Hyperactivity Disorder," ERIC Clearinghouse, reprinted in LDOnline, www.ldonline.org/article.php?max+20&id=717&loc=24.

Otto, Mary. "With Groups' Help, the Disabled Carve Out a Place at the Altar," in the *Washington Post,* April 3, 2005. www.washingtonpost.com/ac2/wp-dyn/A22073-2005Apr2.html.

Ross-Kidder, Kathleen. "Learning Disabilities, ADHD and Delinquency: Is There a Link?" www.ldonline.org/text.php?max=20&id=995&loc=104.

Ross-Mockaitis, Martha. "Welcoming Each Child," in *Alert,* Presbyterian Church (U.S.A.).

Rubenezer, Ronald. "Stress Management for the Learning Disabled," ERIC Clearinghouse, reprinted in LDOnline, www.ldonline.org/ld_indepth/slef_esteem/eric_stress.html.

Seay, Bob. "Kids and Teens with ADHD Have Fewer Friends," in additudemag.com, www.additudemag.com/ourkids.asp?DEPT_NO=301&SUB_NO=11.

Stein, Lawrence et al. "ADHD, Divorce, and Parental Disagreement about the Diagnosis and Treatment," from *Pediatrics,* www.pediatrics.org.

Webb-Mitchell, Brett. "The Religious Imagination of Children with Disabilities," in *Religious Education,* Spring 1983.

_____. "Let the Children Come: Young People with Disabilities in Church," in *Christian Century,* October 13, 1993.

_____. "Open House: American Family in the Household of God," in *Theology Today,* July 1995.

_____. "Leaving Development Behind and Beginning Pilgrimage," in *Religious Education,* Winter 2001.

_____. "No Longer Strangers and Aliens: Worshiping with People with Disabilities in the Church," in *Worship,* July 2002.

Video/DVD

Misunderstood Minds. Produced by WGBH Boston, available through www.pbs.com, at ShopPBS.

This very helpful 90-minute video (also available in DVD) was the result of a three-year study of five children and youth with learning differences. The ways in which their families struggled to find appropriate and effective treatment and accommodation is very moving. We suggest using this video to introduce the issue of learning disabilities to your education and worship leaders, Christian education and worship committees, or in an adult and/or youth class.